ENCOURAGING WORDS FOR DIAMONDS

By Dr. Mark D. White

ENCOURAGING WORDS FOR DIAMONDS

By Dr. Mark D. White

Diamonds Are Individuals Who have been through the fire, been under life's pressure, and have stayed committed to the place of accomplishment. These are words that God has given me, telling me never to give up!

PSALMS 107:20:
"HE SENT HIS WORD
AND HEALED YOU
AND DELIVERED
YOU FROM ALL
DESTRUCTION."

Forward

Dr. Mark White is a friend and fellow minister that I have personally known for more than 30 years. I have witnessed him handle a variety of situations with a strong will to always glorify the Lord Jesus. In his latest book, "Encouraging Words For Diamonds," He presents timeless truths and profound insights into the process of changing from a lump of coal to the most valuable gem—the Diamond God made you to be. This book is an assortment of the pricey pearls of knowledge he has acquired over the course of his extensive journey. For every reader, this book will act as a daily source of inspiration. What is God doing? The highest and lowest places in life in Christ are explained by Dr. White, giving you insights into your own journey. Supernatural courage and a sense of purpose awaits you behind each chapter heading, buckle up and enjoy the journey!

Prophet Marty Layton
Senior Pastor, Lifepointe Church
Host, "Speak Life with Marty Layton!"
Hendersonville, TN.

Unless otherwise stated, all Scriptures and quotations are taken from the King James Version of the Bible.
ISBN: 9798830148375
Copyright © 2022 by Mark D. White
All publishing rights belong exclusively to Mark D. White and NVIZIBLE Anomaly Publishing of USA.

Cover Design: done by Amanda Chavez
ArcheTelos Consulting,
email: archetelosconsulting@gmail.com

Words can be short, but the meaning long. Life is like the weather; the changes continue on. My fortitude is beyond logic because it's dependent on His Grace, and without His Mercy, some things would not take place. The battle may be the Lord's, but the responsibility of victory is mine. In the midst of each battle, my attitude is what should shine. Even at times, there is remorse for what I want things to be. But having one word in due season defies the logic of what I cannot see!... mdw3114

~

THE FRUIT OF YOUR LIPS COMES FROM THE SEED OF YOUR THOUGHTS!

~

"THE SON OF GOD BECAME A MAN TO ENABLE MEN TO BECOME SONS OF GOD." – C.S. LEWIS.

~

DISCIPLINE STARTS IN YOUR THINKING BEFORE MANIFESTING IN YOUR LIFESTYLE AND REACTIONS TO CIRCUMSTANCES! MDW42722

~

YOU CAN BE DECEIVED IF YOU LOVE PEOPLE MORE THAN YOU LOVE TRUTH! 2THESSALONIANS 2:10-12

~

FROM MARK D. WHITE

Knowledge can come from books, but wisdom comes from experience. With over 50 years in the ministry, I have pastored and been to many nations in Europe and Central and South America. His focus is on helping leaders fulfill their destiny. The price of leaders is to duplicate themselves. We need to do responsible work in raising those to take our place. This book is about years of hearing wisdom from the Holy Spirit to shape coal into a Diamond.

Statement

Suppose you wonder about the numbers at the end of some statements. These are the dates the Spirit of God dropped them in my heart. These are words that God has given me to encourage you to never give up!

PSALMS 107:20: "HE SENT HIS WORD AND HEALED YOU AND DELIVERED YOU FROM ALL DESTRUCTION."

ENDORSEMENTS

From those who have seen and heard Jesus in me!

By Pastor Jimmie Rogers Snow

I have known Brother Mark White for many years. I have a great respect for his anointing and his loyalty to his calling. Mark has proven himself over the years as a true and faithful man of God and a dear friend.

After carefully going through his new book, I was amazed at how he used various statements in a poetic fashion to convey wisdom to his readers. Especially backing it up with chosen scriptures.

If you happen to be an average believer of today, as with the world in chaos as it is. If you happen to be in need of encouragement and strength in this hour. I highly recommend Dr. Mark D. White's new book "Encouraging Words for Diamonds." His book has something for everyone.

Diamonds are jewels made up under pressure; even a pearl is developed from the pressure that's in an oyster from a grain of sand caught in its shell that irritates the muscle, secreting a fluid that helps ease its pain, creating a beautiful pearl as the result.

It was Jesus who delivered the parable of the pearl of great price in the gospel of Matthew. In the book of Malachi, which closes the Old Testament, and Israel returned after 70 years of captivity to the Babylonians. Israel fell back into the same trap of deception and turned from God, but a faithful remnant that stood firm moved God's heart, then he said in Malachi 3:16,17.

> Then they that feared the Lord spake often one to another, and the Lord hearkened, and heard it, and a book of remembrance was written before him for them, that feared the Lord and thought upon His name."

And they shall be mine, saith the Lord of hosts, in that day, when I make up my jewels, and I will spare them, as a man spares his own son, that serveth him. This word Jewels in verse 17 is a Hebrew word and means a special treasure. It's also found in Exodus 19. I believe Brother Mark is conveying, that he wants his readers to be challenged to become Gods special treasure. The wisdom of his writing is backed up with scriptures and Brother Marks years of experience and wisdom.

I highly recommend this book, be sure to get extra copies to give to others.

Jimmie Rodgers Snow
Nashville, Tennessee

By Helen Duplantis

God's word is to be sought after. When the enemy comes against you, he wants you to feel there is no way out of your situation. He tries to make you believe that God is finished with you. As you are tired under pressure you are so low; you have to look up to see bottom. You will begin to call out to God and seek after Him. Then, you begin to see yourself crawling out of that ditch of despair.

This book, Encouraging Words for Diamonds, instructing you in patience and love will help to bring you back to your desired position and even greater to where God has called you. Keep seeking, keep knocking and keep asking. Until you become that precious and shiny stone. Mark, thank you for your faithfulness to God and the body of Christ. I pray that everyone who reads this book will grow deeper into the love and richness of God's word.

Helyn Duplantis - Houma, Louisiana

By Dr. Commodore & Janie Warren

Dr. Mark White is truly a man of God walking in the call of a Prophet. His new book " Encouraging Words for Diamonds" is an example of someone with access to the throne room of God. His revelation will answer many questions about why we go through what we go through to show how good and wonderfully made we are.

Diamonds go through a process, just like the true Sons of God do, but the result is you being a part of God's "diamond squad." This is a must-read for each person destined to work building the Kingdom in these last days.

Dr. Commodore & Janie Warren
Trenton, Tennessee

~

By Prophet Darren & Lydia Canning

Mark D. White is a good friend of mine. I remember walking into a meeting years ago, where I was asked to sit in the front. The only thing was that there were no seats available when I got there, and no preacher wanted to give up a seat for me except Mark. I felt awkward, but Mark put me at ease. He was very humble and let me sit in his spot. His humility drew me to him, and we became friends. This new book will help you understand how to have victory in your life. Too many Christians sit around hoping for

things to happen. Mark speaks about the need to make things happen as you are directed by the hand of God. As you seek Him, you will find Him as you seek Him with all your heart (Jeremiah 29:13). But when the lord gives you a plan, you must act and step out by faith. This book will emphasize this notion; therefore, it has utility in the Kingdom. You will be blessed through Mark's teachings and ministry.

Darren and Lydia Canning
Almonte, Ontario Canada

~

By Pastors Loretta & Dale Toliver

Mark White's new book comes with much pondering and reflection on his own experience in life. He brings a prophetic gifting and Fatherly Guidance to the body of Christ. This book is not intended to promote chasing after prophetic words or supernatural encounters. But to sit down at the feet of Jesus as Mary did and let the encounter happen with her. God's word will be fulfilled through a sold-out and consecrated people. Inside, you will find a challenge to press into God's presence and glory and to cooperate with Him in revealing His love to needy people.

This book encapsulates biblical truth in bringing together the new and old. Matthew 13:52: "Every

Scholar of Scripture who is instructed in the ways of Heavens Kingdom Realm is like a wealthy homeowner with his house filled with treasures new and old." Marks' book is loaded with thought-provoking wisdom, making it more than a 2-hour read. But a workbook that requires thought and reflection to bring a change of heart and more powerful assurance of God's love alive in us. It is our pleasure to recommend Mark White's book to you.

Pastors Dale and Loretta Tolliver
Unlimited Glory Assembly, Wheeler, Illinois

By Dale and Janette Haskett

Dale and I have known Mark for many years and have been so blessed by his ministry. Encouraging Words for Diamonds is full of revelation and prophetic truths. I believe these truths will encourage you and cause you to mature and become the person that you are destined to be.
Dale and Janette Haskett
Unlimited Glory Assembly, Wheeler, Illinois

~

By Bishop Bennie & Tammy Jones

Mark White has been a friend to our family for over 40 years. There has been a fervent hunger and a devoted passion in his life to know God in a more intimate relationship. The reading of this book will compel you to reach for a holy lifestyle which will ultimately lead to the promise of a heavenly reward.

Mark has certainly been through the fires, pressures, and training that life demands throughout the process of living. He is truly a diamond that is used to cut deeply into the hearts of men and women who want to go deeper with God.

We wholeheartedly recommend this book to the body of Christ. This teaching will be life-changing for those who will feast upon the riches of wisdom that will be discovered throughout each chapter. Thank you, Mark, for staying committed to the call.

Bishop Bennie & Tammy Jones
Monroe, Louisiana

By Carmen Y. Santos G.

My name is Carmen Yadira Santos, from Costa Rica, and I met Pastor Mark in Colombia at a Seminar and translated for him.

After reading this book, Pastor Mark, I like the way you write and express yourself. Not only revelations and great knowledge and wisdom but shows your life experiences that demonstrate the trials of your life and the jewel that you are and have become with an open heart to share it with others, proving that love conquers all...

This is a truly amazing book! It is like a book of wisdom, self-examination, and meditation in one's life, past, present, and future. All are based in the Word, and the guidance through the wisdom that you use, ideas, and sayings are incredible. Like a book of proverbs... enlightening, refreshing, and true.

It is an eye-opener. It makes you really do a self-examination of how are stand with the Lord, what we do and not do, how we live, right out wrong...

Tools to least how to deal with our weakness and increase in faith and good deeds. Really a MDW practical bible

Carmen Y. Santos G

PSALMS 107:20: "HE SENT HIS WORD AND HEALED YOU AND DELIVERED YOU FROM ALL DESTRUCTION."

Introduction

Life is full of ups and downs; while we ride the rollercoaster of life, there are times when we find ourselves in a quandary. There is pressure in life and from those we need in our lives and those that we wonder why they say what they do.

In this book, we speak prophetically and just commonsense words of wisdom. But out of it all, we shared our hearts and what we needed to hear, and others needed me to share. I pray this book has gold buried deep, and you find that pressure with time and fire can turn coal into a diamond.

The time it takes to grow in wisdom is what it takes to go through life experiences. The fairness of life varies based on calling, skill, desire, and education. Everything in life is not about your moment but about your eternity. Everything you will be reading is to encourage you, motivate you to look at your life, and thank God you are still alive at the reading of this forward.

For His Purpose

Mark D. White

PSALMS 107:20: "HE SENT HIS WORD AND HEALED YOU AND DELIVERED YOU FROM ALL DESTRUCTION."

CONTENT

Dedicated To

To the Holy Spirit who gives wisdom to all men freely who seek to know his voice. The Holy Spirit anoints people without an education to lead and change lives and sets the foundations for taking the message and power of Jesus around the world. To friends of my past and friends of my future who believed in me and my purpose. To my children Seth & Pamela, Jordan and granddaughter Evangeline White, Micah Anna Grace, who all have helped me love as Jesus loves!

The Purpose of These Writings

I was at the early age of 15 when I started in the ministry. I was privileged and honored to be an Assembly of God Pastor's son. My dad and mom were James and Anna White; both were excellent examples of servants of God who taught by example. They practiced what he preached. Insight comes from a passion for the wisdom of God, which is given to individuals who have fought the fight and kept their faith in life's challenges.

As time passed and situations were challenging, experiences kept my heart's door open to learning. Knowledge comes from education and books, but wisdom comes from experience. Life comes with responsibility, and the pressure of life shapes one's decisions.

But the words given by the Holy Spirit bring encouragement, motivation, and peace for one to finish and win the race of God's call upon one's life.

One can only run a race alone if one is running against time. Being a father in the natural and being a spiritual father requires you to practice what one preaches. Being a living example is a message often seen but not always heard.

Diamonds are priceless because of what it takes to shape what was used as fuel to burn for energy or warmth. The becoming of beauty is shaped to wear as

decoration has a statement for all eyes to see. The prophetic and apostolic influence amongst the nations comes from proven time-tested experiences, as is a diamond.

This speaks of how they live more than what they can give. Words change lives. A man on one knee with the phrase Will you, creates a complete sentence and paragraph.

These statements are the first impression and the start of another chapter in the book of one's life. Pressure is needed to shape and establish what is desired. Even Jesus learned obedience from his suffering in Hebrews 5:8 and Hebrews 2:10.

Though he was a son, he learned obedience by what he suffered! For it became him, for whom *are* all things, and by whom *are* all things, in bringing many sons unto glory, to make the captain of their salvation perfect through sufferings.
Your desire is to be shaped to be a vessel of honor for God to use you under the pressure of humility and trust in the Holy Spirit. Can you be humble in God's eyes as well as in mankind's?

We find ourselves always being evaluated in our call, results, and purposes. There will always be those who critique you inside and out. The scripture in 1st Corinthians 11:31 tells us to judge ourselves before others judge us. The exact relevance is to forgive ourselves and pursue restoring ourselves also.

THE CHALLENGE IN LIFE IS NOT TO BECOME A CONFORMIST BECAUSE ANYONE CAN BLEND IN, AS IT TAKES A PERSON WITH CONFIDENCE NOT TO CARE IF YOU STAND OUT. FEAR OF WHAT OTHERS MAY THINK IS WITCHCRAFT TO CONTROL US. MDW4822

Being yourself as God sees you is a solid foundation to stand on. Truth is the most relevant, reliable foundation for one to stand on in our daily lives. So, to judge yourself most importantly is in your love relationship with Jesus, His Word, and your attitude of appreciation and honor. Jesus said in

REVELATIONS 2:4: NEVERTHELESS, I HAVE SOMEWHAT AGAINST THEE BECAUSE THOU HAST LEFT THY FIRST LOVE.

~

Evaluate yourself to see if you have lost your 1st love by looking at yourself with your attitude as the primary focus. Are you hungry for the presence of God, do you hunger to read his word, and is your heart filled with worship and praise? Use these things to look and see if you have lost your first love for Jesus! If so, pursue to do these things to renew your first love for Jesus. mdw4622

~

Life is filled with rollercoaster rides as we shape our tomorrow during the difficulties of reaching the end for accomplishment. The scariest thing in life is that

a lifetime of preparation and accomplishments can end suddenly in a moment of wrong moral decisions.

The purpose of accountability is to have relationships with someone who loves you for being you, and they help keep balance in your today. A GOOD FRIEND KEEPS AN ANOMALY FROM TAKING PLACE IN YOUR LIFE. MDW41222

~

Only move quickly with an opinion once you have evaluated the context of what is said or meant to be understood. The Spirit of Discernment is to keep peace and understanding, with unity full of love being the outcome!

~

DIAMONDS ARE INDIVIDUALS WHO HAVE BEEN THROUGH THE FIRE, BEEN UNDER LIFE'S PRESSURE, AND HAVE STAYED COMMITTED TO THE PLACE OF ACCOMPLISHMENT. A LUMP OF COAL IS THE BEGINNING OF A DIAMOND. A PIECE OF COAL CAN BE USED FOR FIRE WHEN IT IS USED FOR A COMMON

PURPOSE. BUT AS YEARS OF PRESSURE
CAN A COAL TURN INTO A DIAMOND.
A DIAMOND'S BEAUTY CAN ALSO CUT
THROUGH THE HARDEST OF METALS!
ALWAYS GUARD YOUR HEART!
KEEPING YOUR ATTITUDE IN CHECK!

IF YOU CAN'T CHANGE THE
MOMENT, YOU CAN CONTROL
YOUR RESPONSE!

Chapter 1
Judged by Fire

Fossil fuels are created from decomposing plants and animals over long periods of time. This is the beginning of what coal & oil are made. Coal can create heat by becoming a fuel for fire that provides comfort in cold weather. Circumstances can determine the purpose and results of coal. Creating a diamond takes continuous pressure and time to change a piece of coal into a valuable diamond.

Over the years, I have prophesied and have known that we will be judged by fire, as stated in 1st Corinthians 3:12-15. This means that we will stand in the presence of God here on earth. His presence is fire.

His presence increases as prayer and worship rise all over the earth. Before you form an opinion of the negative. Our God is a consuming Fire, as stated in Hebrews 12:29, "For our God is a consuming fire." His presence will increase, and the miraculous display of signs and wonders will be released, but the mandate of a change in one's lifestyle will be rearranged in multiple areas.

As the light gets brighter, it gives many fresh vision while opening their eyes to insight and understanding into the future. The blind will have the opportunity to see, and the display of a healing Jesus will be seen every day in public eyes.

As the Glory of God displays signs and wonders, all this will be piercing the resistance and corruption of the world's news media. The undeniable is made known as accountability is sweeping the nations. The scriptures are the roadmap and the balance of what is to be. But the display of love toward Jesus as Lord will change society. Meaningful worship shall increase as God's Glory is released.

I have shared with many leaders that the place of advancement has to do with chapters 15, 16, and 17 of the books of John. We read Moses pleads with God in Exodus 33:18; he seeks God to show him his Glory. Even as Moses is listed as the meekest man on earth, he asks God to reveal His Glory beyond average. You and I shall see Heaven poured out as a public display of God's Glory in our lifetime.

ISAIAH 66:16: "FOR BY FIRE AND BY HIS SWORD WILL THE LORD PLEAD WITH ALL FLESH: AND THE SLAIN OF THE LORD SHALL BE MANY."

~

This is the Word God gave me for you!

The Spirit of God told me that you, individually, are now entering the days of identity. You will cast your vote on what you are and who you are. Your action shall bring judgment or favor. If you do nothing, you will be judged, as stated in James 4:17.

James 5:14 tells us to pray one for another to be healed, and all nations need to be healed (2 Chronicles 7:14). But passion is at war with passiveness, hot with cold, and both against lukewarm. You are entering the valley of decision; Joel 3:14-16.

You will be known amongst angels and demons, and your life will be changed. Jesus said in Revelations 3:11 for you to not let no man take your crown, meaning your influence, authority, destiny, purpose, and calling.

PROCRASTINATION IS THE DOOR TO DEVASTATION,

but the truth is the sword of the Spirit. Hold the shield of faith and let the world know God has an army, and together we stand. WWG1WGA...

DISCIPLINE STARTS IN YOUR THINKING BEFORE MANIFESTING IN YOUR LIFESTYLE AND REACTIONS TO CIRCUMSTANCES! MDW42722

All things in life have meaning and purpose when you trust Jesus. Proverbs 3:5,6: "Trust in the LORD with all thine heart and lean not unto thy own understanding. In all thy ways acknowledge him, and he shall direct thy paths."

~

FIGHT TO CONTROL YOUR RESPONSE IN YOUR SITUATION...GOD IS AT WORK...DO NOT BE THE PUPPET OF CIRCUMSTANCES! MDW22522

~

A PERSON WHO LIES TO THEMSELVES WILL LIE TO EVERYBODY ELSE!

~

CHOICES ARE THE AUTHORITY OF RESISTANCE OR COMPLIANCE, A FOLLOW OR LEAD MINDSET. LEAD BY EXAMPLE WHILE PEOPLE WATCH YOU AS AN EXAMPLE OF JESUS.

~

WORSHIP IS WHEN YOU FORGET YOURSELF AND EVERYTHING AROUND YOU AND ONLY FOCUS ON JESUS.

~

THOUGH OUR DAYS ARE NUMBERED, IT'S UP TO US HOW IN THEM WE'LL SPEND, FOR IF WE SQUANDER OUR TIME, HOW CAN WE TELL OTHERS ABOUT HIM? MDW1285

~

WORDS CAN BE SHORT, BUT THE MEANING IS LONG; LIFE IS LIKE THE

WEATHER; THE CHANGES CONTINUE;
MY FORTITUDE IS BEYOND LOGIC
BECAUSE IT'S DEPENDENT ON HIS GRACE,
AND WITHOUT HIS MERCY, SOME
THINGS WOULD NOT TAKE PLACE... THE
BATTLE MAY BE THE LORD'S, BUT THE
RESPONSIBILITY OF VICTORY IS MINE.
DURING EACH BATTLE, MY ATTITUDE
SHOULD SHINE; SOMETIMES, THERE IS
REMORSE FOR WHAT I WANT THINGS
TO BE. HAVING JUST ONE WORD IN DUE
SEASON DEFIES THE LOGIC OF WHAT I
CANNOT SEE... MDW3114.

~

TO LEARN THE WAYS OF GOD, YOU
MUST LEARN THE LANGUAGE OF
HEAVEN.

~

SILENCE IS NOT LOVING OTHERS. LOVE
IS, I CARE ABOUT YOUR TOMORROW.
GO TO CHURCH...SOME PEOPLE NEED
YOU THERE!

~

A CHALLENGE IN LIFE IS NOT TO
BECOME A CONFORMIST... ANYONE CAN
BLEND IN....IT TAKES CONFIDENCE NOT
TO CARE IF YOU STAND OUT. FEAR OF
WHAT OTHERS MAY THINK IS

WITCHCRAFT TO CONTROL US.
MDW4822

~

Evaluate yourself to see if you have lost your 1st love by looking at yourself with your attitude as the primary focus. Are you hungry for the presence of God, do you hunger to read his word, and is your heart filled with worship and praise? Use these things to look and see if you have lost your 1st love for Jesus! If so, pursue to do these things to renew your first love for Jesus. mdw4622

~

My eternity is not based on obeying any government. Your eternity and my eternity are based on our submission to the Holy Spirit. Acts 5:29 Peter and the other apostles replied: "We must obey God rather than human beings! Daniel prayed, and it was against the law to pray. This put Daniel in the Lion's den. What an honor to be put in jail for preaching the gospel. Acts 4:19 Peter and John's response to the government's control was whether it be right in the sight of God to hearken unto men more than unto God. This you need to judge.

~

THE POWER OF CHOICE IS SOMETIMES A FORCED ISSUE, AND YOU MAKE YOURSELF OVERRIDE FEELINGS TO FOCUS ON RESPONSIBILITY AND RESULTS; IF I LET EMOTIONS CONTROL MY ACTIONS, THEN I CAN NEGLECT THE TRUTH... IF I DON'T DO MY PART... SOME WILL NOT BE HEALED OR GO TO

HEAVEN... I MUST REMEMBER MY
PURPOSE TO ENCOURAGE PURSUIT.

~

LIFE IS FULL OF OPPORTUNITIES, BUT
ONLY CHOICES OPEN DOORS...CHOOSE
GOD'S. MDW31022

~

EXCUSES NEVER ANSWER THE QUESTION;
COMMITMENT IS A CHOICE, NOT A
FEELING!

WHAT YOU COMPROMISE TO GET, YOU
ULTIMATELY LOSE!

PSALMS 107:20:
"HE SENT HIS WORD
AND HEALED YOU AND
DELIVERED YOU
FROM ALL
DESTRUCTION."

Chapter 2
Dreams & Desires United

This is from chapter 10, "Knowing Destiny Hinges on Pursuit," from our book "Time the Unfound Friend." Time is like an infant, though it grows, and changes happen without oversight. As with a child, they will grow and change into something different than your dream, desire, and acceptance identity.

Being a good manager, parent, or steward is being responsible in guarding as you would protect a child. Being successful has no minimal or maximum time limit. Success wants to spend as much time as possible being the unconscionable, intimate, passionate investment to bring an outcome without restraint or limits in success.

Desires are an acronym for unconscionable pursuits. These desires and dreams must often be guarded, guided, and grounded in foundational truths. The integrity of the heart is the place to start.

As stated by Polonius in Hamlet, "to thine own self be true." Starting right does not guarantee to end with the same motive as you started with.

As stated by King David in Proverbs 4:23, to his son Solomon for him to guard his heart tells Solomon to protect the integrity in his own heart. Life is shaped and created as destiny hinges on how one pursues daily affairs.

~

THE TRUTH IS, WHAT YOU COMPROMISE TO GET, YOU ULTIMATELY LOSE.

~

As Paul, the Apostle, wrote in First Timothy 6:10 that the "Love of Money" is the root of all evil. It's not about money, but the love of it, the craving, passionate desire for fulfillment that money can create. Ecclesiastes 10:19 tells us that "money answers all things." This can be so true on many issues.

~

WHEN MONEY TAKES THE PLACE OF TRUST, ONE'S INTEGRITY AND EVEN RESPECT LOSE POWER IN LIFE.

~

RELATIONSHIPS ARE DESTROYED WHEN BUILT AROUND MONEY. THE OLD SAYING IS, "A RICH MAN CAN BUY FRIENDS, BUT A POOR MAN CAN BORROW THEM."

~

DESTINY CAN HAVE ATTRIBUTES WITH THE IMPORTANCE OF TIME. THE ISSUE

OF WHAT IS INVESTED CREATES A RETURN.

~

As stated in Galatians 6:8, "Those that make provision for the indulgence of fleshly fulfilling appetites and passions shall experience the rewards of corruption." The keyword here is balance; believe me, it is like time; it can be hard to find. Management is as much an investment in your relationship with time as a work schedule could be overwhelming. Without the word balance, a marriage can be destroyed, health can be depleted, and money can disappear. It's like the old statement,

"WHEN YOUR OUTPUT IS MORE THAN YOUR INPUT, YOUR OUTPUT IS YOUR DOWNFALL."

~

It's like gaining a degree from a university; it requires research, study, and then application. Destiny is hinged upon pursuits; a diploma in undergraduate or a master's degree in a specific category involves a sacrifice of time in several areas as an investment in others. The divided time can be a landslide as issues accumulate and the weight and responsibility increase. One of my professors at the University of Phoenix taught me a statement I will never forget.

"YOU DO WHAT YOU CAN DO, DELEGATE WHAT YOU CAN DELEGATE,

DELAY WHAT YOU HAVE TO, AND THEN
DELETE THE REST."

~

Destiny often comes with the purpose of creation, as listed in Psalms 139:13-18 or Jeremiah 1:5. Destiny is an opportunity, but destiny is hinged on pursuit. Even if a child is born a prodigy in music, it still takes the pursuit of sitting at the keyboard of a piano or the strings of a violin. For gifts to come forth, one learns the details of precision and excellence in playing such music as Mozart or Beethoven. mdw91913

KNOW THAT THE DESIRES OF OUR PAST
HELP SET THE PATTERNS OF OUR
PRESENT. MDW9122013

~

WHAT IS IMPORTANT IN LIFE IS NOT
HOW YOU ENTER BUT HOW YOU EXIT
THIS EARTH INTO ETERNITY. MDW41919

~

Seasons of Change - This is the season for the opportunist, as in the waiting of many to see what is next or the fear of some to preserve and protect. Procrastination will cause many things to go undone. But those led by the Holy Spirit, your battle is already won. So, as the Spirit of God leads, prepare to take great strides into new territories to receive. Walking on water starts with one step at a time. 101811

~

Hebrews 6:12 tells us of the required working of faith and patience to receive the promises of God. I find people with no patience have no faith, for without patience, you have no peace, and in the resolve, you have no anticipation with joy. Galatians 5:6 says faith works by love, and 1st Corinthians 13:4-8 says love believes the best.

SOMETIMES, THERE ARE PEOPLE WITH SHORT TEMPERS WHO HAVE LITTLE LOVE, LITTLE PEACE, AND LITTLE PATIENCE AND NEED MUCH TIME WITH GOD. MDW41814

~

Faith without peace is weak faith. Faith that has peace puts trust in the Prince of Peace. Keeping one's thinking controlled is as in Isaiah 26:3. Keep your mind on Him, and He will keep you in peace!

~

Proverbs 3:5 tells us to trust in the Lord and lean not to our own understanding. This requires you to commit your way and trust God! In I John 5:14, this is the confidence we have in Him if we ask anything according to His will, we know He hears us, and we have the petitions of our heart...mdw41714.

The weatherman is prophesying and predicting the coming atmosphere, and nothing happens. It seems the weather is blowing over. Also are the Suddenlies of God taking place, as it requires faith not to be passive but aggressive. Overcoming fear is necessary to overcome and prevent attacks.

While hearing the whisper of the wind declaring it is time for corporate action of churches to stop the powers of darkness. To prevent, restrain, and destroy the plans against the people of God. It is time for the unseen to manifest, to wake up the sleeping giant called the body of Christ.

BELIEVING IN THE SUPERNATURAL POWER OF GOD IS TO BE EXPECTING THE MIRACULOUS TO BE PART OF YOUR EVERYDAY MOMENT...MDW11419.

~

BEING AN OVERCOMER COMES FROM THE INSIDE OUT; HAVING CONFIDENCE THE GREATER ONE IS IN YOU!

~

Forgiving yourself is a requirement for Jesus said to love your neighbor as you love yourself in Matthew 22:34-40. To forgive others is a response of forgiveness toward yourself. The aspect of Romans 8:1 of no condemnation requires you to walk in the spirit and not your flesh. To be at peace with yourself is to see beyond your moment or your past.

Chapter 3
Commitment Beyond Choice!

There are many options and opportunities in life. In the book of Ecclesiastes 9:10,11, the prophet speaks by experience. [10] Whatsoever thy hand findeth to do, do it with thy might; for there is no work, device, knowledge, or wisdom in the grave, whither thou goest.[11] I returned, and saw under the sun, that the race is not to the swift, nor the battle to the strong, neither yet bread to the wise, nor yet riches to men of understanding, nor yet favor to men of skill; but time and chance happens to them all.

No matter what is going on in your life. The sunsets and rises without your consent. Life is what you make it; the ability to change often starts with what you speak about and desire.

~

CHOICE IS A VOICE!

~

I CAN HEAR YOU AS I SEE YOU ON WHOSE IS ON THE LORDS' SIDE.

We find ourselves speaking with our body language, from our eyes and facial expressions to nervous fidgeting. In the William Shakespeare play Hamlet, Act 3, Scene 1. Hamlet makes this statement that resonates around the world. "To be, or not to be" that is the question. What do you want in life? Do you recreate your past or create your future? Are your emotions a ride on a rollercoaster of up and down? Who is in charge of your today? We know the footsteps of the righteous led by the Lord as stated in Psalms 37:23-24. 23 The Lord orders the steps of a good man, and he delights in his way. 24 Though he falls, he shall not be utterly cast down: for the LORD upholds him with his hand.

~

SOMETIMES, PRAYER CANNOT STOP THE MOUTH FROM WHAT IT SAYS. LEARN TO FORGIVE, FORGET, AND JUDGE ONE'S ATTITUDE. LOVE

~

FAITH IS NOT A FEELING BUT A CHOICE. MDW72123

~

Whoever is in charge of your today is in charge of your tomorrow (Romans 6:12). Creation happens from your words, thoughts, and actions. Victims are those who cannot get up when knocked down.

Victors can get up and keep trying to win and overcome the moment, no matter how hard it seems. Quitters never win, and winners never quit!

~

THE CHOICES WE MAKE ARE THE HARVEST WE CREATE!

~

YOU HAVE AN ASSIGNMENT, A PURSUIT OF DESTINY. THE ONLY QUESTION IS, ARE YOU WILLING TO PAY THE PRICE REQUIRED FOR ACCOMPLISHMENT?

~

GOING TO SCHOOL TO BE A DOCTOR IS COSTLY IN TIME AND RESPONSIBILITY. THE EXCESSIVE PRICE OF TIME WITH THE INVESTMENT IN KNOWLEDGE ASSIMILATION REQUIRES COMMITMENT. THEN, THE EFFORT TO HELP OTHERS AND MAINTAIN STANDARDS FOR HUMANITY'S HEALTH AND WELL-BEING IS VERY COSTLY.

~

ONLY THOSE WHOSE HEART AGREES WITH THE CALLING PAY THE PRICE FOR EXCELLENCE.

~

FROM THE EFFORTS OF A MECHANIC TO THE NECESSITY AND COMMITMENT OF ENGINEERS COMES THE DESIGNING OF A BETTER CAR, A BRIDGE, A SKYSCRAPER, OR MACHINERY THAT MAKES ELECTRICITY.

~

FOR HUMANITY TO PROSPER,
INDIVIDUALS MUST SUCCEED.

~

THE CALLING AND EQUIPPING ARE LIKE
BREATHING AND EXHALING. YOU
CANNOT DO ONE WITHOUT THE
OTHER; BOTH ARE NEEDED TO LIVE
LONG AND PROSPER.

~

THE ANOINTING IN THE MARKETPLACE
OF THIS WORLD IS JUST AS CRUCIAL AS
THE ANOINTING IN BUILDING THE
KINGDOM OF GOD IN THE TABERNACLE
OF THE LOCAL CHURCH.

~

RESPONSIBILITY
GIVEN REQUIRES EFFORTS MADE.

~

I TAUGHT MY CHILDREN, "IF YOU
DON'T TRY, YOU HAVE ALREADY
FAILED."

~

Isaiah 1:19,20 [19] If ye be willing and obedient, ye shall eat the good of the land: [20] But if ye refuse and rebel, ye shall be devoured with the sword: for the mouth of the Lord hath spoken it.

~

THOSE WHO PROCRASTINATE WALK
PAST THE DOOR OF OPPORTUNITY!

~

SUCCESS BEGINS IN THE UNSEEN BEFORE IT'S EVER SEEN!

~

If your imagination cannot see possibilities, it sees hopelessness. I have used this phrase throughout my ministry to strengthen my decision of faith and logic concerning knowing God's will for my life and ministry.

~

OBEDIENCE IS THE PRIMER TO THE FLOW OF SUPPLY OF ALL YOU HAVE NEED OF!

~

IF YOU HAVE TO TALK YOURSELF INTO SOMETHING, YOU CAN TALK YOURSELF OUT OF IT! BUT WHEN IT'S GOD'S WILL, YOU DON'T HAVE TO TALK YOURSELF INTO IT, AND YOU CAN'T TALK YOURSELF OUT OF IT!

~

FOCUS AND COMMITMENT ARE THE TWO REQUIRED STEPS NEEDED FOR SUCCESS!

~

1. There is never an option to obedience to God's word!
2. There is never an option to be patient!
3. There is never a commitment option!
4. There is never an option for integrity!
5. There is never an option to tell the truth!
6. There is never an option to tell a lie!

7. There is never an option to reading your Bible!
8. There is never an option to seek God!
9. There is never an option to live by faith!
10. There is never an option to being a Sower!
11. There is never an option to forgive!
12. There is never an option to love like God!

~

WORDS ARE CHEAP, BUT ACTIONS ARE EXPENSIVE!

~

THE ACTION OF OUR FAITH PERMANENTLY SECURES OUR TOMORROW!

~

KNOW THIS! IF YOU LIVE OFF OF EXCUSES, YOU WILL DIE BECAUSE OF THE REASONS!

~

EXCUSES ARE THE BACKBONE OF SLOTHFULNESS!

~

TRUTH SEPARATES EXCUSES FROM PROCRASTINATION!

~

GOOD INTENTIONS WERE NEVER INTENDED TO BE FORGOTTEN!

~

AN IDLE MIND IS THE DEVIL'S WORKSHOP!

~

IF SATAN CAN MANIPULATE YOUR EMOTIONS, HE WILL MANIPULATE YOUR LIFESTYLE!

~

LIFE IS WHAT YOU MAKE IT; YOU CHOOSE THAT YOURSELF!

~

THE LEVEL OF AUTHORITY YOU DESIRE TO WALK IN WILL BE THE LEVEL OF AUTHORITY YOU MUST SUBMIT TO!

~

A LEADER WILL ONLY LEAD AS FAR AS FEAR FOLLOWS THEM!

~

WITCHCRAFT IS MANIPULATION, INTIMIDATION, AND CONTROL!

~

THE DEVIL WILL SEDUCE, SEDATE, AND ENSNARE YOU TO CONTROL YOUR LIFE!

~

KNOW THAT REJECTION IS CONTROLLED BY FEAR OF WHAT OTHERS MIGHT THINK.

~

REJECTION CHALLENGES ONE'S SELF-WORTH AND ABILITIES.

~

THE LAST TEMPTATION THAT JESUS HAD TO OVERCOME WAS REJECTION AS

HE CRIED OUT ON THE CROSS, "ELI, ELI,
LAMA SABACHTHANI? MEANING, MY
GOD, MY GOD, WHY HAVE YOU
FORSAKEN ME? THIS IS FROM MATTHEW
27:47 AND FULFILLS PSALMS 22:1
~
PASSION IS NOT AN EMOTION BUT AN
UNSEEN DRIVE IN ONESELF TO GET,
PURSUE, AND ACCOMPLISH.
~
FAITH AND FEAR ARE TWO POWERFUL
FORCES. BOTH HAVE THE ABILITY TO
CREATE SOMETHING OUT OF NOTHING
AND BRING INTO EXISTENCE THAT
WHICH DOES NOT EXIST!
~
FAITH AND FEELINGS CAN BE LIKE
TWINS, LOOKING ALIKE ON THE
OUTSIDE BUT DIFFERENT ON THE INSIDE.
FAITH IS A COMMITMENT TO WHAT
GOD'S WORD SAYS, WHERE EMOTIONS
ARE CO-DEPENDENT ON WHAT IT SEEMS
AND WHAT WE WANT.
~
THE FIGHT OF FAITH DOES NOT ALLOW
MANIPULATION BASED ON THE
OPINIONS OF OTHERS. WE STAND ON
THE WORD OF GOD.

PSALMS 107:20:
"HE SENT HIS WORD AND HEALED YOU AND DELIVERED YOU FROM ALL DESTRUCTION."

Chapter 4
The Power of Purpose

1ˢᵀ JOHN 3:8B FOR THIS PURPOSE THE SON OF GOD WAS MANIFESTED, THAT HE MIGHT DESTROY THE WORKS OF THE DEVIL.

~

Purpose is a determination of an accomplishment or intention. Some need to comprehend this little understanding that Influence is the power of creating tomorrow. The problem is, are you the one influenced or the one taking the lead? Is it possible you are affected as a follower with blind trust in those you follow?

The Power of Purpose is stated in Proverbs 29:18: "Where there is no vision, there is no pursuit." So, I ask you, what is your purpose today, your goal, your plans, your greatest desires?

The key to promotion is discipline, which is the statement of results. Results are the corresponding action to pursue consciousness or unconsciousness. The power of choice is set in motion before one makes even the very effort of discipline or being slothful and negligent. Even the subconscious desires between males and females are the act of reproduction because of our hormonal subconscious.

A lack of self-discipline has allowed millions of humans to die because of selfish desires. This statement is written in the history of one of the greatest servants on earth. "Poverty is cruel and sad that a child must die so you can live how you wish, Mother Teresa." If you support abortion personally or support someone who supports abortion, the blood of each child is in your hands!

Christine Tomlinson made some wonderful statements as follows. You don't just live on purpose; you purpose to live. Your life has a great purpose. Before God formed you in the womb, He knew you. Before you were born, He set you apart. God created you on purpose, in His image. He made you to live with purpose.

So many people are looking for a purpose in their lives but do not even know what purpose is. If you understand what you are looking for, then you can find it. Your purpose is intentional, determination, and a resolution. It is an intention that guides your actions.

Purpose is not just a noun. It is a verb. God purposed that we live out His kingdom. Because

God is love, and we are the happiest when we are loving and being loved. Purpose, as a verb, brings hope. It means to be determined to do something. Purpose to see what He has for you.

Every moment has a purpose. Even if you know your purpose, you have to become proactive. What does God intend for you? Purpose to fulfill all He has for you today.

People are in your life for seasons and reasons. There are three types of friends. There are those you choose and, those that choose you, and those that God puts in your life. The ones who choose you mostly use you, but the ones you prefer fill the voids and make a difference in life's enjoyment. But the ones that God chooses and puts in your life are for the strength of your tomorrow, motivate you today, and encourage you to expedite your positioning for destiny. Romans 8:28

~

GOD NEVER WASTES WORDS, TIME, OR POWER. EVERYTHING HE DOES HAS A PURPOSE!

~

MATTHEW 20:26, WHOEVER WANTS TO BECOME GREAT AMONGST YOU MUST BE YOUR SERVANT!

~

MATTHEW 25:40 VERILY I SAY UNTO YOU, IN AS MUCH AS YE HAVE DONE IT

UNTO ONE OF THE LEAST OF THESE, MY
BRETHREN, YE HAVE DONE IT UNTO ME.
~
THE MANDATE OF GOD IS YOUR
OBEDIENCE! MDW11722
~
YOU HAVE GOT TO TRY TO DO
SOMETHING TO GET SOMETHING DONE!
~
PEACE IS A RESULT OF CONQUERING THE
WORKS OF YOUR ENEMY. COMPROMISE
LIMITS PEACE AND JOY BASED ON THE
AGREEMENT OF YOUR ENEMY.
~
THERE IS PASSION, AND THERE IS
PASSIVE.
~
THERE IS NEVER A JEZEBEL WITHOUT
THERE BEING AN AHAB. WHILE KEEPING
PEACE SEEMS TO REQUIRE PASSIVENESS,
THE PASSION FOR PEACE IS
COMPROMISED.

JESUS SAID IN REVELATIONS THAT HE
WANTS YOU HOT OR COLD. LUKEWARM
IS PASSIVE AND INDIFFERENT!
~
WHEN YOUR LIFE SEEMS TO BE IN THE
WILDERNESS IS WHEN YOU ARE
TRUSTING GOD; WHEN YOU ARE ON

THE MOUNTAINTOP IS WHEN GOD TRUSTS YOU!

~

PROCRASTINATION CAN CAUSE YOU TO MISS THE DOOR OF OPPORTUNITY!

~

WALKING ON WATER IS BASED ON TRUSTING WHAT YOU BELIEVE IN YOURSELF AND HOW MUCH YOU BELIEVE THE WORD OF GOD!

~

FEAR IS SELF-PRESERVATION, AND PRIDE IS SELF-ELEVATION.

~

LAUGHTER IS PROOF OF PEACE, JOY, AND CONFIDENCE AS LIFE CHALLENGES US!

~

IT IS EASY TO LAUGH WHEN YOU HAVE NOTHING TO HIDE, NOTHING TO FEAR, NO MATTER THE PROBLEMS, AND ARE NOT CONTROLLED BY OTHERS AND CIRCUMSTANCES. LAUGHTER IS WHEN YOU ENJOY LIFE!

~

AN OPINION IS AN OPTION OF CHOICE!

~

WHEN YOU KNOW NOT HOW TO PRAY, YOU PRAY IN THE SPIRIT! ROMANS 8:26,27

HERE ARE THE BENEFITS PRAYING

IN TONGUES!

1. Tongues are the entrance into the supernatural.
2. Tongues are the prayer in the New Testament.
3. Tongues are a direct line to talking to God.
4. Tongues are a language demons cannot understand.
5. Tongues are the believer's direct access to the throne room.
6. Tongues are speaking divine mysteries.
7. Tongues are drawing secrets to life's complicated issues.
8. Tongues are prophesying your God-ordained future.
9. Tongues are praying out God's plan for your life.
10. Tongues are knowledge, counsel, and secrets withheld from the wicked.
11. Tongues are the entrance into the realm of the spirit – the miraculous zone.
12. Tongues strengthen your inner man with might.
13. Tongues keep you spiritually fit.
14. Tongues are praying for things that have been hidden to be revealed and made known.
15. Tongues are decreeing the secrets of God.
16. Tongues pull you from the past into the future.
17. Tongues build improvement and are a source of spiritual edification.
18. Tongues build a strong, solid premise to carry the anointing.
19. Tongues build-up and stimulate your faith.

20. Tongues give you unstoppable progress that your enemies cannot deny.
21. Tongues give praise and thanksgiving unto God.
22. Tongues line you up with the divine will of God.
23. Tongues are speaking the language and will of God.
24. Tongues help with your ultimate weakness.
25. Tongues are the ultimate assistance to prayer.
26. Tongues qualify all things to work for your good.
27. Tongues render you to be God-minded.
28. Tongues make you miracle minded.
29. Tongues magnify God.
30. Tongues enlarge your perspective of God's potency in your life.
31. Tongues give spiritual refreshing and rest.
32. Tongues hone your sharpness and accuracy in the anointing.
33. Tongues facilitate the entrance into the gifts of the Spirit.
34. Tongues equip you for the wonders of God.
35. Tongues are fine-tuning and sensitizing your spirit man to the voice of God.

~

THERE IS A RELEASE OF HOLY GHOST POWER IN PRAYING IN TONGUES!

~

The prophet speaks in Hosea 4:6 about how God's people are destroyed for lack of knowledge. It is amazing how we find zealous people for the presence of God in a meeting but choose to overlook the key to the door that opens the Heavenlies.

Around the world, there is a language commonly called the Heavenly language, prayer language, also known as praying in the Spirit or speaking in other tongues. In this teaching, I want to stir you to listen to the Christ in you, also known as the Holy Spirit, on the precise ways of praying in the Spirit.

There are three ways of praying in the Spirit, as each has a distinct purpose in seeking God in receiving answers to prayer. There are ways of worship in the common language of one's environment worldwide. Singing and praying in the Spirit is not for understanding at times.
One of the ways of praying in the Spirit is Speaking in Tongues, as happened in Acts 2:1-4.

A person's dimension in the presence of God has to do with communication from you and to you. Remember that Jesus said in John 10:27 my sheep know my voice. I want you to understand that praying in the Spirit is vital to the supernatural.

Worshipping in tongues is a powerful key for entering into the presence of God in opening the heavens to release the will of God and His power. Your words are the sword of the spirit, as stated in Ephesians 6, in destroying the forces of darkness. The simplicity of growing in the things of God is co-dependent on a relationship with the Holy Spirit, as stated in 2nd Corinthians 13:14, as this prophetic statement is set in motion as you read the message from Apostle Paul.

2 Corinthians 13:14: "The grace of the Lord Jesus Christ, the love of God, and the communion of the Holy Ghost, *be* with you all. Amen.

The word communion in Greek is Koinonia, which means relationship and fellowship. In 1st John, 2:20 tells us we have an unction a stirring inside of us from the Holy One, who teaches us all things. This is the work of the Holy Spirit. It can be challenging to have a strong, lasting relationship with someone with knowledge of the person and their ways of seeing and doing things.

Your prayer life is the bonding of a relationship in knowing the Spirit of God in you, in knowing God's will, and in learning God's ways of doing things. Psalms 103:7 tells us Moses knew God's ways, and the children of Israel only knew the acts of God.

There is so much to cover in building a relationship with the one who created you and the one who paid the price for your eternal redemption from the results of sin. Sin separates you from God and all that He has for you. The blood of Jesus covers one's past, but the precious Holy Spirit takes you into your future in the things of God.

PSALMS 107:20:
"HE SENT HIS WORD
AND HEALED YOU
AND DELIVERED
YOU FROM ALL
DESTRUCTION."

Chapter 5
Leadership In the
Making

THE POWER OF LEADERSHIP WILL BE
DISPLAYED IN ATTITUDE BEFORE
ACTION.
~
CONFIDENCE IS A STEP FORWARD,
WHILE CAUTION IS STANDING STILL,
WHILE FEAR IS A STEP BACKWARD.
MDW42522
~
A LEADER WILL ONLY LEAD AS FAR AS
FEAR FOLLOWS HIM!
~
THERE IS ONLY ONE THING TO DO
TODAY, AND THAT IS TO CREATE
MOMENTS THAT LAST FOREVER!
MDW9615
~

THERE IS ONLY ONE THING TO DO, AND
THAT IS TO DECIDE WHAT TO DO WITH
THE TIME GIVEN TO YOU. J.R.R. TOKIN

~

Again, I tell you, people are in your life for
seasons and reasons. There are three types of
friends: those you choose, those who choose you,
and those God puts in your life. The ones who
choose you mostly use you, but the ones you choose
fill the voids and make a difference in life's
enjoyment. But the ones that God chooses and puts
in your life are for the strength of your tomorrow,
motivate your today, comfort your past, and
expedite your positioning for destiny. mdw83111

~

BUT AS PEOPLE ARE IN YOUR LIFE FOR
SEASONS AND REASONS, THERE IS
ALWAYS A PURPOSE.

~

GOD WANTS TO GIVE YOU ACCESS TO
EXCESS! MDW121295

~

A LEADER WILL STAND IN THE GAP TO
FILL THE GAP AND NOT CREATE A LACK
OF UNDERSTANDING WITH NEGATIVE
EXPECTATIONS.

~

Communication starts with body language and then
actions. The step of faith starts with standing in
faith with a heart of expectation. Knowing what is
around you and what is trying to come to you is
perception-based, as you are listening inside
yourself as you process what others expect.

There is safety in the multitude of counsel, as stated in Proverbs 11:14. But selecting wisdom from panic has to start inside oneself. As stated, Romans 8:14 tells us who are led by the Holy Spirit are strong in leadership.

The presence of the Holy Spirit does not bring a quiet atmosphere of indifference and apathy. But a focus on following steps to worship and obedience based on your relationship with Jesus and his word. The footsteps of the righteous are led by the lord, as said in Psalms 37:23.

~

LIFE IS FULL OF CHOICES THAT ALTER YOUR THINKING. IF YOU NEVER LISTEN TO YOUR CRITICS, YOU NEVER HAVE TO WORRY ABOUT BEING CRITICIZED.

~

Your ability to love your neighbor is based on your ability to love yourself. As Jesus said in Matthew 22:37-40, love your neighbor as you love yourself. The truth may not always be given in love, but it must be received with love. God loves you, and He sees the truth. mdw3818

~

WHAT YOU COMPROMISE TO GET, YOU WILL ULTIMATELY LOSE.

~

ONLY THE PURE IN HEART SHALL SEE GOD. THERE IS NO SEPARATION OF

CHURCH AND STATE. IF YOU LET THE
STATE HAVE THE FINAL SAY, THEN THE
CHURCH HAS LOST ITS PURPOSE.
GOVERNMENT IS PROVEN DARKNESS, SO
DO YOU WANT DARKNESS TO CONTROL
LIGHT? MDW7719

~

AGAIN, I TELL YOU...EVERYTHING IN
THE KINGDOM OF GOD IS ABOUT JESUS,
BUT EVERYTHING IN JESUS IS ABOUT
YOU. MDW82716

~

DON'T WALK PAST YOUR FUTURE
BECAUSE OF THE STUBBORNNESS OF
YOUR PAST.

~

THE PURPOSE OF TOMORROW IS TO BE
FULFILLED TODAY, SO YOU HAVE TO
START NOW! MDW11707

~

TO BE USED GREATLY, YOU HAVE TO BE
CONVICTED GREATLY! MDW53187

~

THE WORST THING TO HAPPEN IS TO
SUCCEED PUBLICLY WHILE FAILING
PRIVATELY!

~

TIME IS SHORT; ETERNITY IS AT HAND; IF YOU WERE JUDGED, WHERE WOULD YOU STAND?

~

IF PRIDE IS IN THE ATTITUDE OF LEADERSHIP, IT IS LIKE A HELIUM BALLOON WITH TOO MUCH AIR. LIFE EXPLODES THEN. BUT NOT ENOUGH HELIUM; YOU CAN'T GET OFF THE GROUND.

~

IF YOU CAN ENDURE PAIN, YOU CAN DEVELOP STRENGTH! BUT NEVER LET PAIN GET MORE VITAL THAN THE MUSCLES ON YOUR FACE. SPEAK THE WORD OF GOD, DECLARE HIS PROMISES!

~

I AM GLAD YOU HAVE LEARNED THAT OTHER PEOPLE'S THOUGHTS DO NOT CONTROL YOUR ACTIONS!

~

THE SAFEST COMMITMENT IS TO LOVE TRUTH MORE THAN YOU LOVE PEOPLE! IF YOU LOVE PEOPLE MORE THAN YOU LOVE TRUTH, THEN YOU CAN BE PERSUADED TO BELIEVE A LIE.

~

A RACE THAT IS NOT RUN CANNOT BE WON. LEAVE A LEGACY AND DUPLICATE

YOURSELF. MAKE DISCIPLES REPRODUCE;
THE SKILLS AND WISDOM OF THE
ANOINTING ARE DEVELOPED IN THE
CALL OF GOD ON ONE'S LIFE; IT IS NOT
YOURS TO HIDE. WHEN PEOPLE RETIRE
AND DO NOT FEED, THE FIRE OF THEIR
DESIRED VISION EXPIRES, AND DESTINY
IS NOT FULFILLED. 42519
~DOING THE WORK OF JESUS BY
PRECEPT AND EXAMPLE SHOULD BE THE
LIFESTYLE OF EVERY CHRISTIAN.

~

Your next season will defy logic:

✓ the undeniable

✓ the undefiable

✓ the unrestrainable

✓ the unexplainable

POWER OF GOD IN YOUR LIFE!

~

In Genesis 1:2, the statement is made of the Spirit of God hovering over the waters of the deep to bring forth the creation of land and all creation. This action of the time invested is the answer to bringing forth change in one's life. Spending time in the presence of God is the start of answering all prayers made in one's life.

Chapter 6
The Power of Love

I Have always said that the proof of love is that it protects what it loves. A person, a pet, an item, no matter what is valued, letting go of it is letting go of love or what you have bonded with. This display was given when God turned his back on Jesus as that which was his only beloved son became sin, and God had to let go of him to fulfill the purpose of Love. There is no greater love than laying down your life for someone.

~

LOVE LOVES TO GIVE, LOVES TO PROTECT, LOVES TO EMBRACE, LOVES TO SHARE, AND LOVES TO BE LOVED!

~

The test of love is forgiveness. The depth of love is commitment and the depth of one's relationship with Jesus and His Word. I can do all things through Christ, who has given me an unlimited ability. When Jesus said to bring the sacrifice of praise, it has to surpass our feelings to a higher level in our commitments.

~

Jesus told us to love our neighbor as we love ourselves, telling us the first of all the commandments *is*, Hear, O Israel; The Lord our God is one Lord: Mark 12:28-30 And thou shalt love the Lord thy God with all thy heart, and with all thy soul, and with all thy mind, and with all thy strength: this is the first commandment. Mark 12:31 And the second is like, namely this, Thou shalt love thy neighbor as thyself. There is none other commandment greater than these. The same is also stated in Luke 10:27

~

IF YOU ARE WAITING FOR FEELINGS BEFORE COMMITMENT, I QUESTION IF YOU ARE A PERSON OF PRINCIPLE.

~

HE ANSWERED AND SAID, " 'YOU SHALL LOVE THE LORD YOUR GOD WITH ALL YOUR HEART, WITH ALL YOUR SOUL, WITH ALL YOUR STRENGTH, AND WITH ALL YOUR MIND,' AND 'YOUR NEIGHBOR AS YOURSELF."

~

If Satan or circumstances can control your feelings, then we are puppets to the strings of others and situations controlling us and our choices. Your choices are the most powerful creative force on earth.

~

During WW2, there was a man named Victor Frankel; Victor commented about his being in a German Prison Camp during World War II, as all prisoners were living with fleas, lice, starvation, and mental and physical abuse. He watches many of his people die as the German soldiers tried to destroy the Jewish people inside and out. He proposed to himself that they can control my surroundings, but they cannot control what I think.

When love is the beat of your heart, it is like the old children's rhyme. Sticks and Stones may break my bones, but words can never harm me. I am sure you know that the power of influence is in the eyes of those full of love. So, understand that love protects what it loves. So, I ask you, do you believe in the power of love?

~

The greatest challenge is loving like Jesus, forgiving like Jesus, having patience, and still expecting the best like Jesus. Believe me, we walk by faith, seeing beyond logic; faith works by love, seeing beyond the moment.

~

WHEN THE THOUGHT OF SOMEONE
MAKES YOU SMILE, PAUSE, AND ENJOY
THE MOMENT.

~

WE WALK BY FAITH... IF WE DON'T SEE
BY FAITH, WE STUMBLE.
OVER WHAT WE DON'T SEE!

~

GALATIANS 5:6 "TELLS US THAT FAITH WORKS BY LOVE."

~

THE ONE THING THAT MAKES TOMORROW IS THE RESOLVE OF ONE'S TODAY. TOMORROW NEVER COMES IF IT IS A REPEAT OF TODAY!

~

At the end of one's day, make sure there is no unforgiveness or neglect in one's heart concerning the truth. The truth is, to be like Jesus, you must learn to love like Jesus!

Bitterness is unfulfilled revenge! Guard your heart and keep in check your attitude about what happened or did not happen. Be bigger than other people's problems. So, let God work in you so that He might work through you! There are times when you need to distance yourself from a pessimist. Being an optimist is having faith in God's faithfulness!

~

YOUR GREATEST ACT OF KINDNESS IS TO SPEAK THE TRUTH!

~

The ones that can handle the truth will stay with you, but the ones that do not like the truth will disappear. Deceiving spirits can sound like love; and act like love but do not care about your eternity; their selfish ways, so do not rock their boat: Sink it!

~

NOTHING CAN BE CORRECTED IF A LIE IS PERPETUATED TO PROTECT SOMEONE'S FEELINGS. SPEAK THE TRUTH IN LOVE AND LOVE EVERY MINUTE OF IT. IF YOU CANNOT HANDLE THE TRUTH, THE SPIRIT OF TRUTH WILL NOT LET YOU INTO HEAVEN.

~

"CARNAL CHRISTIANS ARE LIKE GRAVITY, ALWAYS TRYING TO PULL YOU DOWN. SPIRITUAL CHRISTIANS ARE LIKE THE WIND (RUACH), ALWAYS LIFTING YOU UP."

~

AN OPTIMIST ALWAYS ANGERS A PESSIMIST.

~

REMEMBER, A WIDE MOUTH IS ALWAYS FOLLOWED BY A NARROW MIND.

~

HE THAT SLINGS MUD LOSES GROUND!

~

THE FRUIT OF YOUR LIPS COMES FROM THE SEED OF YOUR THOUGHTS!

~

WHAT YOU COMPROMISE TO GET, YOU CAN ULTIMATELY LOSE.

~

GOD HAS GIVEN LOVE FOR ALL SEASONS!

1. AGAPE' FOR YOUR FUTURE!

2. PHILEO FOR TODAY!

3. STORAGE' FOR YOUR PAST!

4. EROS FOR THE MOMENT!

~

THE HOLY SPIRIT CAN SHAPE YOUR HEART WITH THE FINGER OF A CHILD! MDW71509

~

FAITH IS AN ATTITUDE THAT WORKS BY LOVE, WALKS BY PATIENCE, DISPLAYS PEACE, AND ANTICIPATES WITH JOY! MDW42920

~

Luke 10:19 tells us of the authority that Jesus has given the believer: a believer has accepted Jesus as the son of God, and you receive him as your Lord and Savior. In Mark 12:31, Jesus says to love your neighbor as you love yourself.

All the authority Jesus gave us is co-dependent on faith in having trust in God and His Word. Trust is an attitude of faith that is co-dependent on love. To love yourself is to trust and believe in yourself; as Jesus said, love your neighbor as you "Love Yourself."

~

GALATIANS 5:6 TELLS US THAT FAITH WORKS BY LOVE. LOVING YOUR

NEIGHBOR AS YOURSELF IS BASED ON CONFIDENCE, TRUST, PEACE, AND JOY. THAT IS WHY WE STATED THAT FAITH IS AN ATTITUDE WHICH WORKS BY LOVE, WALKS BY PATIENCE, DISPLAYS PEACE, AND ANTICIPATES WITH JOY!

~

YOUR TOMORROW IS SHAPED BY YOUR TODAY. REMEMBER, WHAT YOU SOW IS WHAT YOU WILL REAP!

~

1st John 4:17-21 tells us that perfect love casts out all fear and that there is no fear in love. The strength of perfect love is based on trust and confidence. Not only do we develop confidence and trust as love becomes mature and committed. We find a level of peace because our relationship is based on experience in giving and receiving. Philippians 1:6 tells us of confidence based on what God starts God finishes.

Even the fruit of the Spirit listed in Galatians 5:22-23 gives a layout of expectancy of what comes out of your roots called character, expectancy, and ability. Every fruit of the spirit has a responsibility, a commitment, and a purpose.

The old phrase of seeing is believing has to do with faith, expecting, and yielding to the anointing as the anointing is God's ability in you, as said in

Philippians 4:13: "I can do all things through Christ (the anointing) who enables, strengthens me."

~

AS IS THE ROOT, SO IS THE FRUIT!

PSALMS 107:20: "HE SENT HIS WORD AND HEALED YOU AND DELIVERED YOU FROM ALL DESTRUCTION."

Chapter 7
Never Abort One's Destiny

HERE IS MY OPINION ON ABORTION!
IF YOU SUPPORT A BABY NOT TAKING ITS FIRST BREATH, I SUPPORT YOU TAKING YOUR LAST!

~

Words can be short... but the meaning is long... life is like the weather; the changes continue no matter what... my fortitude is beyond logic because it's dependent on His Grace, and without His Mercy, some things would not take place... the battle may be the Lords, but the responsibility of victory is mine... in the midst of each battle my attitude is what should shine... at times there is remorse for what I want things to be... having just one word in due season defies the logic of what I cannot see... mdw3114

It is amazing how many people abort their destiny because of frustration and lack of patience. The scripture says in Isaiah 40:31 that those that wait on the Lord shall renew their strength; they shall run and not be weary and walk and not faint. It is very specific about walking and not fainting. Time is the key to the door of accomplishment; time invested and time being patient requires control of one's emotions. Quitters never win, and winners never quit.

~

PROPHECY IS NOT ALWAYS YOUR ANSWER, AND DESTINY IS NOT A CHOICE!

~

If Satan can manipulate your emotions, He will manipulate your lifestyle. So, casting down imaginations and bringing every thought to the obedience of Christ, which is God's presence. mdw72410

~

CHOICE IS THE CREATOR OF CHANGE. SOME THINGS IN LIFE YOU WILL CONQUER, BUT ONLY BY THE COMPLICATED POWER OF CHOICE. YOU HAVE TO MAKE YOURSELF DO WHAT'S RIGHT!

~

IN ALL YOU KNOW AND DO. YOUR
CONSCIENCE IS THE CHOICE OF YOUR
ETERNITY. SO, WALK, AND NOT RUN,
AND SEEK GOD TO UNDERSTAND HOW
YOU CAN FOLLOW AND LEAD. AS ALL
EYES ARE ON YOU! MDW71617

~

Desperation can bring one to the place of cooperation or manipulation when needing a miracle. Faith has it now, but now never diverts from patience, and when you have done it all, you still stand till prayer is visibly answered. Remember that the fruit of your lips comes from the seed of your thoughts!

~

FEED YOUR DESIRES, NOT JUST YOUR
NEEDS; DESIRES FILTER AND GROW
WEAK IF NOT FED. YOU ARE REDEEMED
BY THE BLOOD OF THE LAMB!
PSALMS 107:2 - 107:20

~

NEEDS CRY FOR THEMSELVES AS DESIRES
HAVE TO BE LISTENED TO, TO BE HEARD.

~

FIGHTING THE GOOD FIGHT OF FAITH IS
NOT A FEELING BUT A RESPONSE IF
YOUR NEEDS CRY LOUDER THAN YOUR
DESIRES AND DREAMS. KEEP ONE'S
FOCUS BEYOND EXISTENCE, NOT JUST

FULFILLMENT ACCOMPLISHMENTS, AND SUCCESS WILL COME IN TIME.

~

DREAM BIG, SEE FAR, AND FIGHT HARD. DON'T QUIT. FEED YOUR DESIRE THAT YOUR HOPE WILL INSPIRE OTHERS TO SEE HOW BIG AND POWERFUL GOD IS! DISPLAY THE POWERFUL LOVE OF JESUS...

~

TRUST IS LIKE YOUR NEXT BREATH; YOU DO IT WITHOUT THINKING! MDW71117

~

TO BE AN OPTIMIST, YOU MUST BE AN OPPORTUNIST AGAINST OPPOSITION! MDW22297

~

IF YOU CAN SET FIVE MINUTES IN MOTION, YOU CAN CHANGE YOUR LEVEL OF AMBITION AND DEVOTION! 102497

~

IF YOU LIVE BY EXCUSES, YOU CAN DIE BECAUSE OF THE REASONS!

~

TIME IS SHORT, AND ETERNITY IS LONG; IF YOU WERE JUDGED RIGHT NOW, WHERE WOULD YOU BELONG?

~

THE PURPOSE OF THE FRUIT OF THE SPIRIT IS NOT HOW I TREAT PEOPLE BUT HOW I TREAT THE HOLY SPIRIT!

~

PATIENCE IS THE STRENGTH OF MY TOMORROW. PATIENCE IS THE HOPE OF MY FUTURE, THE DREAM OF MY DESIRES. FOR WITHOUT PATIENCE, I HAVE NO PEACE. IT IS WITH FAITH AND PATIENCE THAT WE OBTAIN THE PROMISE. HEBREWS 6:12

~

PATIENCE IS NOT JUST A FRAME OF MIND BUT AN ATTITUDE MAINTAINED OVER TIME!

~

IF YOU THINK I AM HEAVENLY-MINDED AND I GOT MY HEAD IN THE CLOUDS. IT IS BECAUSE I CANNOT LIVE ON YOUR LEVEL AND WALK ON WATER AT THE SAME TIME!

~

COAL UNDER PRESSURE FOR YEARS IS COMPRESSED INTO A DIAMOND!

~
IF YOU ARE IN THE MIDDLE OF
NOWHERE, WHERE DO YOU GO, TO GO
SOMEWHERE?

PSALMS 107:20: "HE SENT HIS WORD AND HEALED YOU AND DELIVERED YOU FROM ALL DESTRUCTION."

Chapter 8
Listening to Lighting

DOES LIGHTING FLASH IN THE TWINKLING OF THE EYE AND THEN IS FORGOTTEN WHILE STILL LOOKING AT THE SKY?

~

Hearing God's voice is one of the most imperative commitments one can have in their life. We compare the words of the Holy Spirit as if what he speaks and how we comprehend comes as lighting.

For a brief moment, the light flashes inside you to hear or see what the Holy Spirit is saying, and then it is gone. Hearing the Holy Spirit's voice is as essential as breathing or the necessity of water.

Jesus said in John 10:27, "My sheep hear my voice, and I know them, and they follow me." Knowing the voice of the Holy Spirit is knowing Jesus in person. In a simple way to put it, the Spirit of Truth leads you on the path of righteousness.

~

YOUR CONSCIENCE IS THE ULTIMATE VOICE OF ETERNITY. NO VOICE SHOULD SPEAK LOUDER THAN A PERSON'S CONSCIENCE. YOUR CONSCIENCE GETS AND KEEPS YOU IN THE PERFECT WILL OF GOD. MDW53012

~

It can be hard to be thankful for those you do not appreciate! To those married, be on guard as your body does not belong to you; it is in dispute. Jesus bought it with his blood, but while you are on earth and married, your wife or husband has a level of influence on it; your mate owns you.

You are a new creation, and you gave up your right to vent or express the voice of the old carnal man, which is murmuring. So, keep the praises flowing and keep planting the seeds of the heart of God.

To those who are single, keep your heart pure so that you might endure the temptations of life. Keep your life active so that you will not be distracted from the presence of the King. Know that He is jealous of your love. So, declare who He is and what He has done to change lives and win battles. Married or single, let it be known that Jesus is your Lord, and He sits on your heart's throne. mdw71014

~

I prophesy that this will come to pass from this point on. In the days to come and the years to be, we shall see Acts 19:20 manifest in our lives. A victorious church is emerging, and no antichrist spirit will prevail, for a revival is here and growing against all powers of darkness, as their resistance cannot and will not prevail.

Triumphant in persecutions and victorious over death we be. No weapon formed against us shall prosper because the Blood of the Lamb has never-ending results. We have overcome by the Blood of the Lamb and the words of our testimony. WE ARE IN CHRIST; He is the light. mdw7513

What can be said when we dread confronting what needs to be? The love in one's heart always starts to remove the enemy's hand. But the choices one makes cannot be regulated when our children give place to the influence of the darkness. A shout of a warning like thunder have we said, does it still not resonate to alter the path which we can dread?

God, open my babies' eyes and let them see. The face value of what is done is in contrast to eternity. So, the prayer of faith we continue to pray. While we plead the blood to keep demons away, as we are trusting God at times seems so hard to do, reminding God that's my baby while forgetting the same thing we have been through too. For God remembers the prayers your mama and dad so often prayed for you. mdw6152014

~

The dinner plate is ready, and the food is hot off the stove. Fine China is on the table, while no doubt a special night. The rumbling is happening as chairs are seated with people in place. The hands are on the table joined as we prepare to say grace. As all eyes are closed and the noses to the air, the underlying emphasis is Let's eat, and who cares?

~

But the unwritten words on Daddy's and Mama's heart is way back when the day our family started. What we had then, compared to now, is a banquet feast and the blessings which speak out loud. For grace, we pray over the food said cannot be compared to the appreciation that cannot be read. So, after you eat what appreciations are not said, let expression be given, you ate more than just water and bread... mdw6102014.

~

WHEN SOMEONE OR SOMETHING IS TAKEN FOR GRANTED, DEPRECIATION BEGINS IN VALUE BECAUSE THE VALUE OF ONE IS NOT OPENLY APPRECIATED.

~

RESPECT IS THE STRENGTH OF LOVE, FOR THE FIRST LOVE LOST IS THE SECOND TREATMENT GAINED? MDW10994

~

RESPECT IS PROOF OF WHAT YOU EXPECT!

~

COMMITMENT SHOULD NOT BE RULED BY OBLIGATION BUT BY DESIRE AND DISPLAY OF ONE'S HEART! MDW9894

~

TOLERANCE IS THE CURSE OF VICTORY! MDW121796

~

THE DEVIL CAN NEVER CONTROL WHAT YOU DO IF HE CAN'T INFLUENCE WHAT YOU THINK! MDW112096

~

YOU ARE RESPONSIBLE FOR YOUR CHOICES. EVEN WITH THE LACK OF UNDERSTANDING, YOU STILL HAVE THE RESPONSIBILITY OF CHOICES!

~

THE HARD PART OF ETERNITY IS EVERYBODY WILL NOT ENJOY IT!

~

JOY IS A MIXTURE OF THE PAST, PRESENT, AND FUTURE. JOY IS HOPE, JOY ANTICIPATES, JOY HAS ENDURANCE, AND JOY IS STRENGTH. JOEL 1:12

~

LAUGH AT THE DEVIL AND HIS PLOY; MAKE YOUR FAITH STRONGER THAN

YOUR MOMENT. JAMES 1:2,3. "MY
BRETHREN, COUNT IT ALL JOY WHEN
YE FALL INTO DIVERS' TEMPTATIONS;
KNOWING THIS, THAT THE TRYING OF
YOUR FAITH WORKETH PATIENCE."

~

IF YOU THINK I'M TOO HEAVENLY-
MINDED AND I GOT MY HEAD IN THE
CLOUDS. IT IS BECAUSE I CANNOT LIVE
ON YOUR LEVEL AND WALK ON WATER.
MDW6522

~

Fighting symptoms of sickness is like fighting
polluted air. It must be filtered in your thoughts,
words, and actions. Faith has a standard beyond
logic, for it is the attitude of Heaven, and confidence
is expectations of God's word fulfilled. Pain tries to
make faith weak and one's thoughts double-
minded.

Your stubborn will can resist or comply. I would
rather die in faith than comply with the works of the
devil. He steals hope and makes one weary. The
power of agreement is imperative in some
situations. Fight the good fight of faith.

~

LET ME GASP FOR AIR AS I TRUST GOD
TO BREATHE INTO ME.

Chapter 9
Do We Fight or
Do We Let?

NO MATTER THE BATTLE, IT'S ALL
ABOUT YOUR RESPONSE!

~

Romans 5:3-5 "And not only so, but we glory in tribulations also: knowing that tribulation worketh patience; And patience, experience; and experience, hope: And hope maketh not ashamed; because the love of God is shed abroad in our hearts by the Holy Ghost which is given unto us."

~

IF WE LET THE VOICE OF OTHERS SPEAK BEYOND OUR CONSCIENCE, WE GIVE UP THE CHOICE OF OUR ETERNITY. I MUST PLEASE THE HOLY SPIRIT, FOR I WANT TO LIVE WITH HIM FOREVER... IF YOU DON'T HAVE A CONSCIENCE, YOU WILL

LIVE IN A HOTTER ENVIRONMENT, AND
GOD WILL NOT LET ME VISIT YOU.
MDW6317

~

The strength of faith is patience; the power of
patience is peace; and the strength of peace is Jesus,
and all of Jesus is love, for faith works by love; I
speak Peace, Peace, Peace to you for the result of
Peace is Joy that cannot be described, for it is joy
unspeakable. For the Joy of the Lord is our strength.
He is celebrating your answered prayers, and I am
with Him!

~

HE THAT THROWS MUD LOSES GROUND!

~

THE PAST HOLDS THE MYSTERIES OF
ONE'S FUTURE.

~

TIME IS SOMETHING PRECIOUS, THOUGH
WE SPEND MORE THAN WE NEED. IF WE
DO NOT SPEND IT WISELY, HOW MANY
LIVES ARE LOST BECAUSE WE DON'T
HAVE TIME TO TOUCH THAT NEED?

~

FOR IF THE SPIRIT OF GOD WAS A
CLOCK, HOW OFTEN WOULD HE STOP
TO TELL US THAT ANOTHER MOMENT
WENT WASTED AND ANOTHER SOUL
JUST WENT TO HELL? MDW1285

~

FOR THO OUR DAYS ARE NUMBERED,
IT'S UP TO US HOW IN THEM WE'LL
SPEND, FOR IF WE SQUANDER OUR TIME,
HOW CAN WE TELL OTHERS OF HIM?
MDW1285

~

IF THROUGH US, THE SAVIOR IS BORN IN
PEOPLE'S HEARTS, YOUNG AND OLD. IS IT
NOT WORTH CONSIDERING HOW MUCH
MORE PRECIOUS OUR DAYS ARE THAN
GOLD? MDW1285?

~

Resisting the devil is more than controlling your thoughts, as stated in Ephesians 6:10-19. Having the helmet of salvation applied is essential, as the shield of faith is just as important as the sword of the spirit. For the sword of the Spirit is the word of God that requires you to respond by declaring God's word to destroy the works of the Devil.

You must be a doer of God's word to resist and attack what the devil sends at you. To speak the word of God is declaring as Job 22:28 tells us to. Life and death are in your tongue, as stated in Proverbs 18:21.

~

IF THE CHURCH HAS OFFENDED YOU, IT
HAS SERVED PART OF ITS PURPOSE. IT IS
THE THRESHING FLOOR THAT
SEPARATES THE WHEAT FROM THE TARE.

~

HOW CAN YOU OVERCOME THE WORLD AND NOT OVERCOME HOW SOME PEOPLE TREAT YOU IN CHURCH?

~

IF YOU CAN'T BE A CHRISTIAN IN CHURCH, HOW CAN YOU BE ONE IN THE WORLD?

~

IF BLOOD DOES NOT FLOW IN THE BODY, THE BODY IS WEAK. IF THE BLOOD OF JESUS DOES NOT FLOW IN THE CHURCH, CHURCHES ARE WEAK.

~

UNFORGIVENESS IS AN ISSUE IN THE CHURCH AND AFFECTS ONE'S ETERNITY.

~

Mark 11:25, 26 [25] And when ye stand praying, forgive, if ye have ought against any: that your Father also which is in heaven may forgive you your trespasses. [26] But if ye do not forgive, neither will your Father which is in heaven forgive your trespasses.

~

SEEDS SOWN IS A HARVEST-GROWN! SEED NOT SOWN IS HARVEST NOT GROWN.

~

BEYOND YOUR SALVATION IS THE DEMONSTRATION OF THE ONE WHO

SAVED YOU, LOVES YOU, AND IS NOW
WORKING ALL THINGS OUT FOR YOUR
GOOD.

~

YOU ARE IN HIS MASTER PLAN BEYOND
WHAT YOU UNDERSTAND. SO, TRUST IS
THE ISSUE. SO, IF YOU CAN TRUST GOD
WITH YOUR ETERNITY, WHY NOT
TRUST HIM WITH YOUR TODAY?
MDW42610

~

TO FORGIVE IS TO FORGET. TO FORGET
IS NOT TO REMEMBER WHAT WAS DONE.
NOW, WHAT WERE WE TALKING ABOUT?
BE BIGGER THAN OTHER PEOPLE'S
PROBLEMS.

~

TELLING OTHERS STARTS WITH
REMINDING ONESELF. MDW41215

~

THE VALUE OF A SEED INCREASES IN THE
VALUE OF THE SOIL. THE SEED ALWAYS
JUDGES THE SOIL!

~

You cannot call it a spirit of conformity, but there is
a false apologetic attitude and yielding to fear of
offending anyone. In Matthew 15:26, Jesus called a
woman a dog, but her desire for her daughter to be
healed was greater than being offended.

What is stronger, your love or your emotional pain? If you are easily offended, you have what is called a chip on your shoulder. Whether from a family member or some stranger, it is about how much of Jesus you can display. If you trip easily or get your feelings hurt and cannot overcome them, are you standing solid on the rock of your salvation?

Go love on your family. Go love on the ones who raised you. Be bigger than other people's problems, be like Jesus, show love and not anger, forgive, and work to forget. No one is worth you going to Hell over. Learn to LOVE like God!

1 Peter 2:7,8: "Unto you therefore which believe He is precious: but unto them which be disobedient, the stone which the builders disallowed, the same is made the head of the corner. A stone of stumbling, and a rock of offense, even to them which stumble at the word, being disobedient."

~

JOY IS A MIXTURE OF ONE'S PAST, PRESENT, AND FUTURE. JOY IS HOPE AND ANTICIPATION. JOY HAS ENDURANCE, AND JOY IS STRENGTH. JOEL 1:12

~

LAUGH AT THE DEVIL AND HIS PLOY. YOUR FAITH IS MORE VITAL THAN YOUR PAIN. THE JOY OF THE LORD IS YOUR STRENGTH, AND LAUGHTER IS MEDICINE!

Chapter 10
Overcoming Emotions

Feelings are the captivating force that can control one's response in life. Emotional or physical feelings can take dominance with pain and laughter. The slightest feeling can reroute directions. Cold or hot, we find the process of self-preservation is compliance to the slightest feelings.

Hope can be challenged, and faith can be doubted, all based on the most deceptive force called feelings, which is the doorbell to deception. Even Jesus addressed emotions in the book of Revelation 3:15, stating that lukewarm is offensive to him. Being hot or cold is yielding of all in choice. But lukewarm is indecisive.

Deception can be a lying Spirit using your emotions to control you! That is why the emphasis on being led by the Holy Spirit, who is also known as the

Spirit of Truth, is a place of lasting victory as an overcomer in life.

~

IF SATAN CAN MANIPULATE YOUR EMOTIONS, HE WILL MANIPULATE YOUR LIFESTYLE. SO, CAST DOWN IMAGINATIONS AND BRING EVERY THOUGHT TO THE OBEDIENCE OF CHRIST. MDW72410

~

Things are not always as they appear, expressively, when we have emotional wounds from our past that have not healed. The importance of what is in Mark 11:25 about forgiveness is a choice in conquering our feelings to fulfill Psalms 107:20

~

IN THE MIDST OF AN EARTHQUAKE IS WHERE YOU LEARN HOW TO STAND! MDW73108

~

FAITH IS AN ATTITUDE WHICH WORKS BY LOVE, WALKS BY PATIENCE, DISPLAYS PEACE, AND ANTICIPATES WITH JOY!

~

YOU HAVE TO RESTRAIN YOURSELF TO RETRAIN YOURSELF TO BE DIFFERENT!

~

A SUDDEN TURN AROUND OFTEN STARES YOU IN THE FACE! MDW5406

~

STRESS CAN POSSESS YOUR TOMORROW
WHILE IT TRIES TO CONTROL YOUR
TODAY!

~

UNDER THE PRESSURE OF LIFE, IT CAN BE
LIKE YOU ARE AT THE BOTTOM OF THE
OCEAN. COME UP FOR AIR JUST TO
CATCH A BREATH EVERY ONCE IN A
WHILE. LEARNING HOW TO RELAX IS A
HEALTHY LIFESTYLE!

~

Years ago, I heard a song about a warrior was a
child. To this day, I still find myself fighting feelings
over circumstances that seem to rob me of joy.

~

FEAR AND FAITH ARE TWO POWER
FORCES, AND BOTH HAVE THE ABILITY
TO CREATE SOMETHING OUT OF
NOTHING AND BRING INTO EXISTENCE
THAT WHICH DOES NOT EXIST!

~

MARK 9:23 TELLS US THAT IF WE CAN
BELIEVE, ALL THINGS ARE POSSIBLE IF
WE CAN BELIEVE.

~

Believing is a verb that means having confidence in
the truth, the existence, or the reliability of
something, although without absolute proof that
one is right in doing so. It is a cognitive process that
leads to convictions. Belief, on the other hand, is a

noun that means mental acceptance of a claim as likely true. It is the act of thinking that something is true, correct, or real. (dictionary.com)

~

Preaching faith is so much easier than living it. There are many people with good hearts but no ability to use their faith or desire to develop their faith. As stated in Romans 10:17, "Faith comes by hearing and hearing by the word of God." I understand why Jesus sent everyone out of the room as he told the little girl who was dead to arise in Matthew 9:18-26

Our emotions can be an anchor to our faith by keeping us from rising higher about the situation. Like all, my love for my dad has brought moments of tears, laughter, and the pastoral input he has given me over the years. There is no difference between believing and knowing. I know my dad would be with Jesus when he dies, but man, these emotions are a challenge in this situation as I stand on the word that my dad will live and not die and will continue to declare the Glory of God.

~

God-given friends are hard to find, really like a miracle. It takes believing in what you cannot see to obtain what God has promised. Be amazed at the moment, which is a great challenge while you believe and speak that you have overcome by the blood of the Lamb and the words of your mouth. I do not share my heart often.

I've not found too many I can trust during 50 years of ministry with my heart. Over the years, friends became strangers, and strangers became friends. Trust is not always given and really must be earned. But my faith is in the lord, and he will wipe my tears, remove my fears, and give me the promise that His word will come to pass. Some teach you to have an imagination in which Christians can ascend in their thoughts, and then there are those with real encounters, visions, and tangible manifestations of God. I would love a visit from Heaven right now, would you? 101817

~

There is a "Season of Change" that happens in everyone's life. This is the season for the opportunist. The waiting of many to see what is next or the fear of some to preserve and protect will cause many things to go undone. But those led by the Holy Spirit, your battle is already won.

So, as the Spirit of God leads, prepare to take great strides into new territories to receive. Walking on water starts with one step! It is your day, hour, and moment to see history change and destiny fulfilled. Allow Jesus Christ to reinvent you & live through you.

~

Peace or Joy requires the strength of Patience. You cannot operate in Faith without Patience. Hebrews 6:12 states that faith & patience work together as the fruit of the Spirit is co-dependent. Temperance is a display of Patience. Meekness, Gentleness, and Goodness requires Patience.112917

~

Patience is the strength of my tomorrow. Patience is the hope of my future, the dream of my desires. For without Patience, I have no Peace. It is with faith and patience that we obtain the promise. (Hebrews 6:12) Patience is not just a frame of mind but an attitude maintained over time.11217

~

FAITH IS AN ATTITUDE THAT WORKS BY LOVE, WALKS BY PATIENCE, DISPLAYS PEACE, AND ANTICIPATES WITH JOY!

~

Fighting symptoms of sickness is like fighting polluted air. It must be filtered in your thoughts, words, and actions. Faith has a standard beyond logic, for it is the attitude of Heaven, and confidence is expectations of God's word fulfilled. Pain tries to make faith weak and thoughts double-minded.

Your stubborn will can resist or comply. I would rather die in faith than comply with the works of the devil. He steals hope and makes one weary. The power of agreement is imperative in some situations. Fight the good fight of faith. Let me gasp for air as I trust God to breathe into me.

~

Chapter 11
The Challenge Is in
The Mirror

GOD IS MORE THAN LOVE; HE IS TRUTH!

I find myself in a quandary looking at love and the protection of what I love. The image of God is always love. But I heard the Holy Spirit tell me to love truth more than to love people. As the statement of the challenge is in the mirror, it is based on what Jesus said to love your neighbor as you love yourself.

If you cannot forgive yourself, it is like picking at a scab on one's body, and healing an external wound takes twice as long. If you pick at the sore, it allows an infection to take hold and the healing to be hindered. In the mirror, it is what you see is what you get. Faith works by love, as stated in Galatians

5:6. Memories are like looking in the mirror last year and preparing for today based on a memory.

~

WE WALK BY FAITH, AND IF WE DON'T SEE BY FAITH, WE STUMBLE OVER WHAT WE DON'T SEE!

~

PIECES OF THE PUZZLE ARE ALWAYS MISSING WHEN YOU'RE NOT LOOKING FOR THE WHOLE PICTURE! FOCUS, KNOW WHAT YOU WANT, NEED, AND DESIRE. KNOWING FEEDS, THE VISION, AND THE VISION FEEDS THE DOOR OF OPPORTUNITY. MDW11711

~

TURN (SET) YOUR EYES UPON JESUS, LOOK FULL INTO HIS WONDERFUL FACE, AND THE THINGS OF THIS EARTH WILL GROW STRANGELY DIM IN THE LIGHT OF HIS GLORY AND GRACE!... MDW112618

~

HOW MANY YEARS LEFT DO WE HAVE? PLEASE DON'T WASTE ANY OF THEM. DON'T DESTROY YOUR FUTURE BECAUSE OF YOUR PAST.

~

Sometimes, prayer cannot stop the mouth from what it says. Learn to forgive, forget, and judge one's own attitude. Love is not always a feeling but a choice. mdw72123

~

Becoming numb to attacks of the enemy will take place as you grow in Christ Jesus. Growing is like outgrowing pants or clothes. How we used to respond doesn't fit anymore, and the pants didn't shrink either! If you insist on wearing the old and still, they don't fit. Suck it up and change your response. 112818

~

I encourage you who are in battle. Walking is harder than running, as stated in Isaiah 40:31, to walk and not faint and run and not be weary. The power of Peace is controlled by the power of patience. In patience is trust and trust in God, as said in Proverbs 3:5

~

TRUST IN THE LORD WITH ALL THINE HEART; AND LEAN NOT UNTO THINE OWN UNDERSTANDING.

~

TRUST IS LIKE BREATHING. YOU DO IT WITHOUT THINKING. THAT IS WHY ISAIAH 9:6,7 TELLS US OF THE PRINCE OF PEACE AND THE INFLUENCE OF HIS GOVERNMENT. THERE SHOULD BE NO LIMIT.

~

Isaiah 9:6,7 For unto us a child is born, unto us a son is given: and the government shall be upon his shoulder: and his name shall be called Wonderful, Counsellor, The mighty God, The everlasting Father, The Prince of Peace.

Of the increase of his government and peace, there shall be no end, upon the throne of David, and upon his kingdom, to order it, and to establish it with judgment and with justice from henceforth even forever. The zeal of the Lord of hosts will perform this.

~

OUR SITUATIONS AFFECT GOD'S INFLUENCE IN OUR LIVES BASED ON FAITH OR FEAR. SO, I PRAY YOU EXPERIENCE THE GRACE TO OVERCOME!

~

These scriptures I recommend you pray often over you and your family and friends.

Isaiah 26:3,4. "Thou wilt keep him in perfect peace, whose mind is stayed on thee: because he trusteth in thee. 4 Trust ye in the LORD forever: for in the LORD JEHOVAH is everlasting strength:"
Psalms 20:6: "Now know I that the LORD saveth his anointed; he will hear him from his holy heaven with the saving strength of his right hand."

Psalms 25 the whole chapter with Psalms 35

Jesus said in John 16:33, "These things I have spoken unto you, that in me ye might have peace. In the world ye shall have tribulation: but be of good cheer; I have overcome the world."

Philippians 4:13: "I can do everything through Christ who enables me."

Psalms 107:20: "He sent his word and healed them, and delivered them from all their destructions."

~

DON'T DESTROY YOUR FUTURE BECAUSE OF YOUR PAST. 112711

~

THE PRICE TO OVERCOME YOUR PAST IS ALREADY PAID IN YOUR FUTURE. GOD HAS FAITH IN YOU!

~

Words of Ruach

The real story is happening in the unseen. The power of love is the power that can open doors, climb mountains, swim rivers, and cross deserts. Do you believe in love? Do you believe it's true? Do you believe in the power of love? Many times, our love has a blind side that others take for granted.

One of the many proofs of love is that it protects what it loves. In a relationship, casual or serious, family or just an acquaintance. Who you are is how you will treat people that you know and don't know! Love is! Love is what?

It is what you want and what you can give. It is who you are and who you want to be. The law of reciprocal is the law of sowing and reaping. For instance, if you cannot look into another person's eyes beyond their past. Your ability to have total peace and joy about that person will be challenged. In this question of the depth of your love, its power, and its purpose. Will it be strong enough to be perfect and the strength to overcome all adversity?

~

THE POWER OF THE UNSEEN CAN BE FELT AND EXPERIENCED.

~

What's the meaning of life? Simply put, it is all about love. One of the greatest hindrances to the power of love is the inability to forgive. Unforgiveness keeps oneself living in the past with the fear of reoccurrence or a repeated situation happening again. When Philippians 3:13-15 explains ability, it also explains inability.

"Brethren, I count not myself to have apprehended: but this one thing I do, forgetting those things which are behind, and reaching forth unto those things which are before," 14 I press toward the mark for the prize of the high calling of God in Christ Jesus. 15 Let us, therefore, as many as being perfect, be thus minded: and if in anything ye be otherwise minded, God shall reveal even this unto you.

~

LOVE IS THE POWER OF INFLUENCE.

~

Ephesians 3:19: "I pray for you to know the love of the Christ which exceeds the ability of logically understanding." Love is more than a feeling; it is the deep strength that causes one to act on impulse and not logic to protect what we love. It causes a commitment of preference for others over oneself. Love is the power that makes one walk with integrity and character and wants others to be filled with laughter and joy. Love is the foundation of patience. Patience is the strength of my tomorrow. Patience is the hope of my future, the dream of my desires.

For without Patience, I have no Peace. It is with faith and patience that we obtain the promise. (Hebrews 6:12) Patience is not just a frame of mind, but an attitude maintained over time. Love is unrestricted without patience.

~

The spirit has a mandate, and the flesh must yield and cooperate for the purpose and the principle of the call of God upon one's life. There has to be hospitality, there has to be love, there has to be seriousness, and there has to be purpose.

~

WHAT YOU SEE CAN SPEAK LOUDER
THAN WHAT YOU HEAR!

~

YOU NEVER BLEND IN UNLESS YOU
WANT TO STAND OUT!

~

WITH DESIRE YOU ACQUIRE, WITH
PURSUIT YOU WILL DO, HOW YOU
MEDITATE IS THE LIFE YOU WILL
REGULATE!

~
THE TREASURE OF AN ATMOSPHERE IS PEACE!

In Genesis 1:2, the statement is made of the Spirit of God hovering over the waters of the deep to bring forth the creation of land and all creation. This action of the time invested is the answer to bringing forth change in one's life. Spending time in the presence of God is the start of answering all prayers made in one's life.

PSALMS 107:20: "HE SENT HIS WORD AND HEALED YOU AND DELIVERED YOU FROM ALL DESTRUCTION."

Chapter 12
Stand Strong with Patience

TIME INVESTED IS THE HOPE OF TOMORROW!

The measure of time invested is the direction of desire and destiny. You must take notice of the cry of your heart to reach the fulfillment of one's soul. This is why Proverbs 4:23 tells us to guard our hearts, for the issues of life come from there. So, stop time and dream! Your consistent thoughts are setting in motion your destiny!

~

WE WALK BY FAITH, AND IF WE DON'T SEE BY FAITH, WE STUMBLE OVER WHAT WE DON'T SEE.

~

PATIENCE IS THE STRENGTH OF MY TOMORROW. PATIENCE IS THE HOPE OF

MY FUTURE, THE DREAM OF MY DESIRES. FOR WITHOUT PATIENCE, I HAVE NO PEACE. IT IS WITH FAITH AND PATIENCE THAT WE OBTAIN THE PROMISE. (HEBREWS 6:12) PATIENCE IS NOT JUST A FRAME OF MIND, BUT AN ATTITUDE MAINTAINED OVER TIME... MDW11217

~

IF SOMEONE APPRECIATED YOU AS MUCH AS THEY USED YOU, YOU WOULD BE TREATED WITH THE HIGHEST RESPECT AND HONOR. MDW11118

~

GOD IS MORE THAN LOVE; HE IS TRUTH.

~

IF I HAVE AN ARGUMENT WITH MY PAST, IS IT BECAUSE I HAVE NOT A PICTURE OF MY FUTURE? WE ALL HAVE A PAST AND HAVE A FUTURE. YOU MAY NOT LIKE WHERE YOU ARE, BUT IF YOU CAN GET PAST THE MOMENT, YOU CAN BEGIN TO LIVE IN YOUR TOMORROW.

~

Below is a prophecy that we had given on October 19, 2008

"These are the days of purging, and is not my Spirit moving throughout the land? To see the sheep and the goats, on what side they would stand. For who is on the Lord's side, and who would decree such a thing? Who will stand up for the God almighty and yield the heart of their whole being? For I'm moving throughout this nation and in accord, you shall begin to see, for there is a violent nation that shall rise up against me. But I, the Lord, shall overcome it, because of the blood of the Lamb, and my Glorious Church shall stand up and will publicly display the I AM with signs and wonders in this nation like never seen before. They are even now perpetually moving to close Satan's door, for I am a God that can lock the door and no man can open it ever again, and I am the God that can open a door and no man can close it again. I have begun an end to the way it was, and I am now starting the process of what I want it to be. So, therefore, who is on the Lord's side, who is going to yield their heart and soul to me? Because I have initiated judgment, and judgment shall stand. So, who will come before me with repentance and cry out for the mercy of God upon this land?"

By Mark D. White

~

FEELINGS CAN CHALLENGE COMMITMENT, BUT WITH PURPOSE, IT SHOULD NEVER BE COMPROMISED. PURPOSE IS THE FOUNDATION OF COMMITMENT. IF YOUR COMMITMENT IS TIRING AND YOU WANT TO QUIT, REMIND YOURSELF OF YOUR PURPOSE. BECAUSE IF YOU DON'T, FEELINGS WILL TRY TO MANIPULATE YOU TO SUBMIT

TO A MOMENT AND NOT CLING TO THE
REASON OF PURPOSE!

I JOHN 3:8: "FOR THIS PURPOSE CAME
THE SON OF GOD, TO DESTROY THE
WORKS OF THE DEVIL!... SINCE YOU'RE
NOT DEAD, THAT MEANS YOU HAVE
NOT FULFILLED YOUR PURPOSE. MANY
ARE CALLED, BUT FEW ARE CHOSEN.
STAY FAITHFUL IN THE LITTLE SO THAT
FATHER CAN REWARD YOU WITH
MUCH. SOME PLANT, SOME WATER, AND
SOME REAP THE HARVEST. WHO ARE
YOU SERVING? YOURSELF OR
GOD...MDW102114

~

FAITH IS AN ATTITUDE THAT WORKS BY
LOVE, WALKS IN PATIENCE, DISPLAYS
PEACE, AND ANTICIPATES WITH JOY.
MDW102118

~

WHEN ONE PROCRASTINATES, ONE
ELIMINATES OPPORTUNITY. THE HOLY
SPIRIT TOLD ME THAT THIS MORNING
IN PRAYER... MDW122018

~

WHEN WALKING ON WATER, DO NOT
TRIP OVER THE WAVES. EVEN WITH UPS
AND DOWNS, YOU CAN STEP OVER
ANYTHING IF YOU FOCUS.

~

SEED IT TILL YOU NEED IT!

~

COMPASSION IS LOVE IN ACTION!

~

REPROGRAMMING IS WHAT GOD WANTS TO DO: TO SEE YOURSELF AS HE SEES YOU. THINKING AS GOD THINKS, SPEAKING AS GOD'S WORD SPEAKS IS THE POWER OF AGREEMENT.

~

LIVING WITH REJECTION CAUSES PITY PARTIES THAT NO ONE IS INVITED TO.

~

YOUR CONSCIENCE SHOULD BE THE LOUDEST VOICE IN YOUR LIFE!

~

To Fight Socialism and Communism is by fighting for your freedom of independence. Expressing yourself is offensive to those who want to control you because they don't want you to have a choice or a voice. They want you to believe the lie, and they are there for your good. Stand out, speak out, and resist PC language.

Your emotions are the old man (meaning your flesh) being controlled by someone else's flesh... I encourage you to resist and overcome the moment to prove the validity of a living God amongst those in the world who fear not Jehovah, the only true God... Scorn the gates of Hell and laugh in the midst of adversity... Offer the sacrifice of Praise even when you do not feel like it. Worship is retaliation against darkness...mdw12312

THE SILENT CHURCH WILL BE INVISIBLE IF THEY DO NOT DISPLAY RESISTANCE AGAINST MANIPULATION, INTIMIDATION, AND CONTROL IS RIGHT. DO NOT YIELD TO WITCHCRAFT!

~

Jesus was on the cross before he was nailed, and he was off the cross before he died. Faith in action is where destiny is. He had risen before the tomb was open, and he knew you before you were born. He is the Alpha and the Omega.

Chapter 13
Anticipation Beyond
Logic

When you listen to religious people, you should never go into a bar or witness or talk to a prostitute on the street corner about Jesus Christ. If what others think of you and your reputation exceeds saving the soul, that is going to hell. You need to stop and listen to the words of Jesus. "In as much as you have done it unto the least of these, you have done it unto me."

Sometimes, someone's eternity should take priority over your moment of what someone else thinks. The only opinion that counts after it is all over is Jesus on judgment day. We all want to hear, "Well done, thou good and faithful servant, enter into the joy of the Lord!" MDW92111

I remember walking into a bar, walking up to a young man, and telling him his name was David.

That freaked him out. I prayed for him, and God changed his life. Faith without works (efforts) is dead.

~

We are seeing and hearing throughout our nation the cry that Shakespeare said of "To Be or Not to Be." What is the truth, and who makes it true? As the government is speaking out in totally divided platforms, we see even in churches a rising up in division over what is truth versus what are opinions of truth. Remember, a half-truth is a whole lie.

To speak boldly, Truth and its influence are in your hands. No one has the Power of Choice more than you. If you are a follower, which most are, I ask you, is it possible the ones who are leading are blinded and misleading people? Make sure error is not coming from your church leadership. Know your Bible!

~

YOU HAVE A CONSCIENCE, AND YOU HAVE THE POWER OF CHOICE.

~

I HAVE TAUGHT AND BELIEVED SIN IN THE PULPIT FILTERS INTO THE PEW. SO ARE THE STANDARDS OF LIVING RIGHT BEFORE GOD'S EYES.

~

THE PARENTS' SINS BECOME THE CHILD'S SINS UNLESS CHOICES ARE MADE TO CHANGE LIFESTYLES.

~

Everything has to be in the arena of Choice. No matter your mother or father or who raised you or even who or what has still influence over you. As Harry S. Truman said, "The Buck Stops Here." You are responsible. The age of accountability is in your hands. You are choosing to follow the baby killers (pro-abortionist) or those that do not compromise a standard of truth.

The truth about a baby is that after three weeks, its heart is beating. Abortion is a human being murdered in the womb while baby whales are protected. This spiritual battle is easily overlooked because of witchcraft in the church and a world of manipulation, intimidation, and control.

No matter what the devil or his kids do or the lies they tell, you are still responsible for the choices you make in doing something or doing nothing. Ignorance is not an excuse when a matter of the heart is the issue. Since "The Inquisition," intimidation has become mental torture, and destruction has become the method of controlling what you say or identify with. There are those who compromise the truth.

Before God, there is no compromise to the truth. Jesus is the only way, and there is none other. No one can lead without being a follower at some time in their life. Someone must influence another, so who is your standard? Can you separate politics from eternity?

Jesus said to render to Caesar what is Caesar's, but your eternity is not under the control of the government (Caesar), or is it? You make the choice. The Power of Choice is the promise of your eternity. Think about it!

~

BRING YOUR EXPECTANCY UP HIGHER...PHILIPPIANS 4:13

~

John 21:25 And there are also many other things which Jesus did, the which, if they are written could, I suppose that even the world itself could not contain the books that should be written about the miracles Jesus did. Amen. There are things you will do for the Kingdom of God, and only God, Jesus, and the Angels will remember.

What the Devil Lucifer forgets God overseas. You are the carrier of the anointing to change lives. Take nothing for granted, and remember you are doing it not to be seen or known of man but doing whatever you do, you are doing for and unto Jesus!

John 14:12-14 (KJV) Verily, verily, I say unto you, He that believeth on me, the works that I do shall he also do; and greater works than these shall he do; because I go unto my Father. Duplicating Jesus starts inside out, not outside in. Purity, holiness,

and integrity are standards; remember that
Matthew 5:8 is the requirement of displaying the
supernatural works of God.

~

AND WHATSOEVER YE SHALL ASK IN MY
NAME, THAT WILL I DO, THAT THE
FATHER MAY BE GLORIFIED IN THE SON.

~

IF YE SHALL ASK ANYTHING IN MY
NAME, I WILL DO IT.

~

THIS IS SHAMEFUL, BUT WE ARE NOT
CLOSE TO A LITTLE BIT OF DOING THE
WORKS OF JESUS.

~

So, desire that you might acquire, and pursue that
you might do... Father, everyone who is reading this,
may they have an encounter with you that changes
their lives forever!

~

IT IS YOUR DAY, YOUR HOUR, YOUR
MOMENT TO SEE HISTORY CHANGE AND
DESTINY FULFILLED...ALLOW JESUS
CHRIST TO REINVENT YOU & LIVE
THROUGH YOU!

~

Hebrews 10:38 The just shall live by faith. God
needs my faith in His faithfulness. Not having faith
in God is accusing Him of lying. Hebrews 11:6
Without faith, you cannot please God. Romans
14:23 What is not faith is sin.

James 1:6-8 double-minded man receives nothing from God. 1st John 5:14, if we have confidence he hears us, we have the petitions of our heart. Romans 10:17 Faith comes by hearing God's word. Jude 20: Praying in the Holy Ghost builds up your faith. Proverbs 3:5: Trust in the Lord with all your heart, and you will receive.

~

Chapter 14
Reputation Creates
Expectation

We, as believers, are to be spirit-led, not letting the blind lead the blind. If you do not know what God's Word says, you are blind; if you do not understand what is God's will you are confused. We find ourselves in a quandary. Taking a stand against your heart is hard, and neither should you.

The old saying is that if history repeats itself, the truth cannot be hidden forever, for our future is codependent on truth. The Holy Spirit is the Spirit of Truth, as stated in John 16:13. It is disturbing when people do not want to hear the truth. But as stated in 2nd Thessalonians, many are deceived because they do not love the truth.

~

The Apostle Paul said in II Thessalonians 2:10b, "Because they received not the love of the truth, that they might be saved." If you are a true leader, you never lead from behind; that is like riding a donkey with you facing where you have been and in the question of where you are going. We have an advantage when we do it in agreement with Jesus. We get to rule and reign in Heaven and eternity, but if you follow the blind, leading the blind. There is a place in the ditch for you.

Being Spirit lead is not following the crowd, nor is it the instigator of rebellion or strife. We are at a close level of war that has never been. These are the last days, and the outpouring of God's power with signs and wonder with miracles happening is our destiny as believers.

But as Moses said, who is on the Lord's side? At that time, if you followed the crowd, you worshiped a cow and rebelled against God, and the earth swallowed them up, or the snakes sent by God bit you. What is your future is your choice; you can say all you want that God is in control. But is He? He is not making your choices but responding to them if you don't take a stand for what is right. Shame on you!

If you support those who kill babies, I will forgive you, but the baby's blood cries out to be held by its own mother. If you do nothing, you have done something. Yep! Giving place to communism, one world government, and the Anti-Christ. Stand for righteousness. Vote for that which exalts Jesus and brings truth to the surface with no lies added. Revelations 22:15... Hope to see you in Heaven.

~

A PERSON OF FAITH IS NOT SOMEONE STUBBORN AND FOOLISH, BUT SOMEONE OF PEACE AND CONFIDENCE THAT ALLOWS PATIENTS TO RULE... MDW111614

~

THERE ARE TWO DAYS LEFT IN THIS YEAR. TODAY AND TOMORROW! I SO MUCH LOOK FORWARD TO LIVING TODAY TOMORROW.

TRUST IS LIKE YOUR NEXT BREATH. YOU DO IT WITHOUT THINKING!... MDW71117

~

CHOOSE YOUR PATH AND WALK TOWARD IT... FAITH MAY FEEL LIKE A VOID, BUT IT SEES BEYOND THE CLOUDS AND CLIMBS ABOVE THE PROBLEMS TO REST IN THE ASSURANCE OF EXPECTANCY ... OUR TRUST IS IN THE LORD...PROVIDES 3:5,6...MDW92717

~

LOVE TRUTH MORE THAN YOU LOVE PEOPLE!

~

GOD IS MUCH MORE THAN LOVE; HE IS TRUTH.

~

As in the story of the frog in the kettle, we have allowed the enemy to have the upper hand. The frog's story in the kettle is what the devil is doing. Suppose the frog is put in the kettle with cold water and then warmed up gradually. The frog adapts till he is cooked. But if the frog were dropped in hot water, it would jump out immediately.

Some people have been peacemakers that are introverts, and now we need to be extroverts. To make peace, you have to be strong in war. If you do not defeat the enemy in the spirit realm, he will try to control your natural domain.

We wrestle not against flesh and blood but against principalities and powers of darkness. The one thing is what you don't do in being a Christian; God sees as much as what you do. For what you do in secret will be brought forth to be seen.

So soon, your prayer life will be made public. You will quit being a closet Christian, for if you do not have a voice, you will lose your choice in what you do to represent your faith in God's faithfulness and the price that Jesus paid for your total salvation.

Many are controlled by a deceiving spirit called apathy. Thinking that God is in control, but He is not if He cannot get you to fast and pray, cry aloud, or sound the alarm. To call meetings together and pray to pull down strongholds that have taken and continue to take our freedom in being bold in our faith and being bold in and about His Word. These are the last days, as you know it. You will either fight, ignite, do what's right, or take flight. But God sees what you are not doing as much as He sees what is being done! 102314

~

Jeremiah 6:16, 17: "Thus saith the Lord, stand ye in the ways, and see, and ask for the old paths, where is a good way and walk therein, and ye shall find rest for your souls. But they said we will not walk therein. 17 Also, I set watchmen over you, saying, Hearken to the sound of the trumpet. But they said we will not listen.

~

Joel 2:15-18 The shadow of one's mind is based upon memories that are only remembered by the light of something else. It is so amazing that as we age as adults, our children or grandchildren bring to light memories that we vaguely remember until someone walks in our shadow following our footsteps... God is so Good...

~

If you never listen to your critics, you never have to worry about being criticized. Your ability to love your neighbor is based on your ability to love yourself. As Jesus said, love your neighbor as you love yourself. The truth may not always be given in love, but it must be received with love. God loves you, and He sees the truth. 3818mdw

~

To those who are married, be on guard. Your body does not belong to you; it's in dispute. Jesus bought it, but while on earth, your wife or husband has to say so about it. You are a new creation, and you gave up your right to vent or express the old man's voice. So, Keep the praises flowing and keep sowing the heart of God.

To those who are single, keep your heart pure so that you might endure the temptations of life. Keep your life active so that you will not be distracted from the presence of the King. Know that He is jealous of your love.

So, declare who He is and what He has done to change lives and win battles. Married or single, let it be known that Jesus is your Lord, and He sits on your heart's throne.71014

~

I am republishing this because it needs to be reread. Personally, I know that because family and friends pressure you to conform to others' ideals and not one's own conscience.

My eternity is based on my conscience and my relationship with Jesus. When I am at the judgment seat, I will be judged for the choices I make, not what others make or try to make for me.

~

Running from a battle is running from victory. Running from what people say about you is running from vindication. Life is full of battles, but victories are only to those who stand on principles of truth, not parallels of people's opinions. Remember, your eternity is based totally on you individually and what you believe, not what others think. So, when you have done all, stand your ground because a smile from Heaven does not remove the frown of carnal men.

~

I choose to believe in a pre-tribulation rapture. I do not control time or seasons, but God does (Acts 1:7). Jesus is coming for those looking for his appearance. With their teaching, no one can produce the actual rapture or no rapture; all they have is just opinions with scriptures conjured together to defend an argument. When the rapture happens, or if it happens, I want to be ready.

I lose nothing believing in Daniel's 70 weeks, the 7-year tribulation, the marriage supper of the lamb, or the pre-tribulation rapture. But if I live as though there is no instant catching away, you live with the sin of presumption, as David mentioned in Psalms 19:13 or Psalms 66:18. If I know of iniquity or wrong in my heart, the Lord will not hear me.

It is not about the twinkling of an eye leaving this earth as much as a breath away or a heartbeat away from leaving this earth. So, ask the question, whether by death or rapture, am I ready to meet God? There are many whose heart is right who are in error and are teaching doctrines of devils.

~

HOLD YOUR LEADERS ACCOUNTABLE TO YOUR BIBLE!

~

So, be cautious; work out your own salvation with fear and trembling (Philippians 2:12). Love the truth more than loving people (2 Thessalonians 2:9-12). No one or their teachings or beliefs are worth going to hell over. 22518

Chapter 15
Irreversible Standards

Is it God's will for the devil to steal from you, kill you or any of your family, or destroy you in any way? You can resist him, and he must flee. You can bind him with the name of Jesus, rebuke him, attack him with the sword of the spirit, using the word of God and holding the shield of faith to resist the things the enemy sends at you.

You are to wear the helmet of salvation, have your loins rapped with the truth, and your feet have the shoes of righteousness. We must fight the good fight of faith, trusting in the Lord.

Having faith in God's faithfulness while counting it all joy when we fall into all types of temptations, knowing the trying of our faith and the power of patience will cause us to lack for nothing. We are overcomers by the blood of the Lamb and the words of our mouth.

So, when you have done all, never surrender to the lies of hell.

The kingdom of Heaven suffers violence, but the violent take it by force. I refuse to surrender my will to demons or those used by demons. I choose to stand on the promises of God and know my redeemed life, for I am redeemed from the hand of the enemy.

For God's plan is for me to be victorious, triumphant, and know he answers prayer, knowing that through faith and patience, I will experience God's promises, for they are yes and amen! If God be for me, who can control me, not my moment and not those who deny the faith of Jesus in me?

I create my future; I refuse to recreate my past. I am a blood-bought child of the King, and no weapon formed against me shall prosper, for the greater one is in me, and if I die in battle, I still win. O grave, where is thy victory and death? Where is thy sting?

My faith in God's faithfulness prevails over the devil's attacks, for I have the name, the blood, and the word of God. I am not a victim but a victor in all my circumstances. So, seek the kingdom of God first, and everything else will be added to you. You can change your moment with faith in God. Never surrender, never give in, and never quit fighting for what God's word says is yours. 122317

~

THE BLOOD OF DEITY CAME UPON MY HUMANITY THAT I MAY LIVE WITH DEITY THROUGHOUT ALL OF ETERNITY... MDW112117

~

THE VOID OF TOMORROW CAN BE FILLED BY THE CHOICES OF TODAY. MDW122317

~

The Holy Spirit said through Paul in II Thessalonians 2:10-12 about many being deceived because they do not love the truth. Deception is the misleading of truth. The chance of a lie being fulfilled is like the chance of the truth never being fulfilled. A half-truth is a whole lie. God cannot lie. Jesus is the spotless lamb; he is the way, the truth, and the life, while the Holy Ghost is the Spirit of Truth.

If you do not know the shepherd's voice, you are in a paradigm shift of choice. The comparison of others can be the pivotal point and shift, which can be the beginning of the misleading of truth. Many will be deceived because it is what they want to believe, as Paul said, heaping unto themselves teacher that scratches itching ears as stated in II Timothy 4:3.

The emotions of the flesh can summon up false realities that can cause the blind to lead the blind, and those who fall into the ditch will find it difficult to get back into the straight and narrow path of righteousness.

The leaven of the Pharisees was a deception to keep misleading the people with partial that the leaders cannot be accountable for their lies. The Holiness of God will purge out the pulpit of many. The Chief Shepherd will not allow the under-shepherds to keep leading His sheep astray.

For John 15 has started with this Jewish new year, the purging and pruning are taking place as stated in I Peter 4:7. The pruning and purging will begin in the leadership of the body of Christ as the presence of God does increase, manifestations of signs and wonders are released as visible encounters with angels will begin and not cease. The war in the heavenlies is over the truth, not control over the earth, because God is alpha and omega.

When Jesus called Satan the father of lies in John 8:44, it is because Satan gave birth to a lie, and there is no truth in a lie other than it's a lie, for a little leaven leavens the whole lump. Except the Lord build the house those that labor; labor in vain as stated in Psalms 127:1.

The Hollywood of ministry will be replaced by the stardom of the overwhelming presence of God, where hours shall turn into days, days turn into weeks, and weeks turn into months.

When the river begins to flow, so shall the sovereignty of God we will see and know. Our days are numbered not in defeat but in the display of God's people taking their seats in the authority of display of who we are and who He is.

The light will increase amid the wars that seem not to cease but will come to a sudden end as men and women of God enter to abide in the Holy of Holies as the body of Christ. We are called to be a triumphant Church. The heavier the anointing, the deeper the revelations.102217 Remember!

~

WHAT YOU COMPROMISE TO GET, YOU CAN ULTIMATELY LOSE.

~

When life is hopeless, you feed your hope; when answers are fleeting, you keep asking questions. When fear is overwhelming, you embrace peace; all this is a moment for the steps of those who refuse to give in and surrender.

Everything in life is set to give opportunity to those who fight to have faith in God's faithfulness, receive a miracle, receive an answer, and rebel against your circumstances.

We are light in the darkness, not in the dark with no light. Jesus is our answer; He cannot lie; his promises are yes and amen. We are overcomers by the blood of the Lamb and the words of our mouth. 102112

~

Seasons of Change - This is the season for the opportunist; the waiting of many to see what is next or the fear of some to preserve and protect will cause many things to go undone. But those led by the Holy Spirit, your battle is already won. So, as the Spirit of God leads, prepare to take great strides into new territories to receive. Walking on water starts with one step! 101811

~

PATIENCE IS THE STRENGTH OF MY TOMORROW. PATIENCE IS THE HOPE OF MY FUTURE, THE DREAM OF MY DESIRES. FOR WITHOUT PATIENCE, I HAVE NO PEACE. IT IS WITH FAITH AND PATIENCE THAT WE OBTAIN THE PROMISE. (HEBREWS 6:12) PATIENCE IS NOT JUST A FRAME OF MIND, BUT AN ATTITUDE MAINTAINED OVER TIME.

~

A race that is not run cannot be won. Leave a legacy and duplicate yourself. Make disciples; reproduce the skill and wisdom of flowing with the Holy Spirit while answering the call of God and not hiding your purpose in this life. When people retire and don't feed their fire, their vision expires, and destiny is not fulfilled. MDW42519

~

YOU HAVE NO LIMITS UNLESS YOU RESTRAIN YOURSELF! MDW43019

~

What happens if light compromises with darkness? What happens if truth compromises with a lie? What happens if right compromises with wrong? What happens if integrity compromises with deception? What happens if health compromises with cancer?

~

GOD DOES NOT COMPROMISE HIMSELF TO GET YOUR LOVE, LIFE, AND FUTURE. GOD STILL NEVER CHANGES! MDW5619

~WE HAVE NO LIMITS UNLESS WE RESTRAIN OURSELVES... MDW3119

PSALMS 107:20:
"HE SENT HIS WORD AND HEALED YOU AND DELIVERED YOU FROM ALL DESTRUCTION."

Chapter 16
Voice of Covenant

Feelings can challenge commitment, but your purpose should never be compromised. Purpose is the foundation of commitment. If your commitment is tired and you are tempted to quit, remind yourself of your purpose. Because if you don't, feelings will try to manipulate you to submitting to a moment and not clinging to the reason of Purpose! James 4:17 tells us that for him that knows to do good and do it not, it is a sin to them.

I John 3:8: "For this purpose came the Son of God, to destroy the works of the devil! Since you're not dead, you have not fulfilled your purpose on this earth. Many are called, but few are chosen. Stay faithful in the little so that Father can reward you with many. Some plant, some water, and some reap the harvest. Who are you serving? The system or God?

Priorities start with preference. There is a responsibility, and there is accountability. But the fulfillment of one's heart is linked to enjoyment, anticipation, and application with acceleration because celebration has come into place because of desired accomplishment. mdw102114

~

A SMILE IS THE BEGINNING OF LAUGHTER. GO TO THE MIRROR AND SMILE; THE DOOR IS NOW OPENED TO LAUGH AT SITUATIONS BECAUSE YOU SEE IN YOU THE HOPE NEEDED TO WIN... MDW102114

~

FAITH IS AN ATTITUDE WHICH WORKS BY LOVE, WALKS IN PATIENCE, DISPLAYS PEACE, AND ANTICIPATES WITH JOY. MDW102118

~

You can only fix something if you discern it needs correction. You cannot stop wrong if you do not have an opinion. You can only promote right if you desire to express your opinion. Paul said in Philippians 1:9 And this I pray, that your love may abound yet more and more in knowledge and in all judgment; How can you stop the Devil by just watching? Do something; light has a voice; it drives back the darkness. If someone is trying to control the truth, it's not God. He is the truth, the way, and the light. Do something! mdw92817

~

PSALMS 84:11 NO GOOD THING WILL HE WITHHOLD FROM THEM THAT WALK UPRIGHTLY... I ENCOURAGE YOU TO KNOW THAT WALKING IS NOT STANDING STILL BUT GOING THE DISTANCE.

~

Keep the faith that Jesus has in you; do not give up or contemplate. He is faithful; this is your year of breakthrough and breakaway. Keep the commitment to your calling as serious as you want your physical heart to keep its beat. Do not stop being a doer of the Word of The Lord.

We walk by faith; we live by faith because He is faithful; as you walk the talk and talk the walk, He will change things in a moment. Continue to walk uprightly and not be ashamed of the Gospel our lives preach. Some of your most incredible converts are hearing you with their eyes!

THE HARD PART OF LIFE IS OVERCOMING THE INFLUENCE OF OUR PAST. OVERCOMING THIS IS ALONE NEEDED TO FREE UP THE FLOW OF OUR FUTURE. MDW10117

~

There are wonderful people in our lives who think they need to help change us. Whether it's wife or husband, family, or friends. God is the only one who can change us into the best we can be. His Holy Spirit is working to change you into His image. So have fun today and know the Potter has His hands on you! 10516

~

A PERSON OF FAITH IS NOT STUBBORN AND FOOLISH BUT OF PEACE AND CONFIDENCE THAT ALLOWS PATIENCE TO RULE. MDW101614

~

IF YOU CANNOT BELIEVE IN YOURSELF, YOU WILL DOUBT YOUR DESTINY. MDW12118

~

THE DISPLAY OF PRIDE IS BEING DEFENSIVE. THE DISPLAY OF CONFIDENCE IS PEACE AND NOTHING TO PROVE. MDW5319

~

FAITH IS AN ATTITUDE WHICH WORKS BY LOVE, WALKS IN PATIENCE, DISPLAYS PEACE, AND ANTICIPATES WITH JOY. MDW102118

~

Words can be short, but the meaning is long. Life is like the weather; the changes continue. My fortitude is beyond logic because it's dependent on His Grace, and without His Mercy, some things would not take place. The battle may be the Lord's, but the responsibility of victory is mine. In the midst of each battle, my attitude is what should shine. At times, there is remorse for what I want things to be. Having just one word in due season defies the logic of what I cannot see! mdw3114

~

THE LOVE OF JESUS WAS SO INTENSE FOR YOU THAT HE ENDURED THE PAIN AND SHAME OF THE CROSS. BECAUSE HIS LOVE WAS GREATER THAN THE WORST OF ALL THAT THE DEVIL COULD GIVE OR DO, YOU ARE LOVED WITHOUT LIMIT. MDW5317

~

WHEN ONE PROCRASTINATES, ONE ELIMINATES OPPORTUNITY. MDW122018

~

The purpose of a mirror is to look forward, not backward; the mirror is for preparation and correction to be your best and accomplish your desires. mdw21919

~

Worship is a key to the miraculous. Worship is an attitude, not a metaphor. Have Holy Communion every day and appreciate your redeemer and His blood shed for you. Psalms 107:20: "He sent His Word to Heal you and Deliver you from all Destruction." mdw33020

~

KNOWING WHAT IS IN FRONT IS NOT AS IMPORTANT AS KNOWING WHAT IS INSIDE. 41320

~

The weather is prophesying that things will never be the same. The Suddenlies of God are taking place, and faith is not passive but aggressive. Overcoming fear is required to overcome and prevent attacks. While hearing the whisper of the wind declaring it's time for corporate action of churches to stop the powers of darkness.

~

Light does not submit to darkness. Jesus set the example in Matthew 4:1-11 at the time Satan was the God of this world. Jesus refused to bow to Satan. When the Government is deceptive and manipulative, be wise as a serpent but harmless as a dove Matthew 10:16. But doves will fight to protect their young. mdw42320

~

Shallow is the water that runs so deep. Dry is the face of those who weep. Small are the steps of those that run. Strong is the love of those who have done wrong. The opposite of wrong is right, and glowing are the eyes of those who were blind. mdw42414

~

Chapter 17
Purpose, Seasons, & Reasons

How are you breathing the Ruach? Do you exhale as much as you inhale the breath of God? Is the air filtered or taken as is? The pneuma is the breath of God, also called Ruach in Hebrew. The Cloud is above you, and the cold and hot resistance has created lighting and thunder. Until there is a manifest direction, the wind will blow until there are changes.

Before the raindrops of anointings begin to fall, we will see into the Ruach to inhale the pneuma. At this time, the lighting will come out of the blood-bough's mouth, for an irrevocable storm is coming for those that can catch the wind to see into the future. The Eagles are coming forth with lighting coming out of their mouths with fire in their eyes and talons to grip the scrolls of the aged. mdw52814

The truth might hurt, but rejection can destroy it. What you take for granted can be taken from you. Trust is not blind love; trust is the hope of integrity in someone. 51119

~

WE NEED FIRE AND PASSION FOR TRUTH
AND HATRED OF A LIE.

~

CHOOSE YOUR PATH AND WALK
TOWARD IT. FAITH MAY FEEL LIKE A
VOID, BUT IT SEES BEYOND THE CLOUDS
AND CLIMBS ABOVE THE PROBLEMS TO
REST IN THE ASSURANCE OF
EXPECTANCE. OUR TRUST IS IN THE
LORD. PROVERBS 3:5,6. MDW92717

~

The final temptation was when Jesus cried out in Matthew 27:46 with these words: "Eli, Eli, Lamasabachthani, that is to say, My God, my God, why hast thou forsaken me? Jesus did everything right and fulfilled every prophecy, as in Psalms 22. But in the end, the Father turned his back on Jesus because he could not stand to see his most beloved suffering when Jesus was not guilty of anything!

Overcoming rejection from those you would die for is the hardest thing Jesus did, and that's the example we need to set as Christian leaders. This reminds me of a childhood poem, "Sticks and stones may break my bones. But words will never harm me". You can do this; Jesus did, and so can you.

"Overcome Rejection," control your thoughts, to control your actions, then pray for those that speak curses against you in or out of the church. John 16:33. You can do all things through Christ, who enables and anoints you. You are an overcomer by the blood of the lamb and the words of your mouth.

You are victorious, Forgive, forget, and never live in regret. 2 Timothy 3:12. The Godly shall suffer persecution. Kenneth E. Hagin said that you must not be too Godly if you're not being persecuted. Acts 5:41

What happens if light compromises with darkness? What happens if truth compromises with a lie? What happens if right compromises wrong? What happens if integrity compromises with deception? What happens if health compromises with cancer? God does not compromise Himself to get your love, life, or future. God still never changes! mdw5619

CHOICES ARE NOT ALWAYS IN OUR HANDS, BUT HOLDING ON OR LETTING GO IS! MDW91517

~

If only we had a voice with confidence and we said what we believed, not suppressing our opinions because of the fear of offending someone. Hypocrisy is not walking in love when you deny what is right— protecting someone's feelings because you live in hindsight instead of foresight.

~

When wrong is accepted, that boldly means that right is rejected. There is a road Jesus described as the straight and narrow. No compromise to the path of eternal life, one direction, living on earth as though you are in heaven. It has been noted that you cannot live in Heaven and disagree with God. An individual named Lucifer and one-third of heaven's angels were evicted and not forgiven.

~

What you continually see is a war between light and darkness. The media can lie and deceive, but the truth will prevail. But the issues are before God will stand, and you will see the Glory Grand before man's eyes. No news media can compare the display of miracles everywhere.

We are entering a move of Jehovah that will not be contained or restrained. The deaf will hear, the blind will see, and Down syndrome will receive public miracles. These are the days of Elijah, and the miracles will overtake all resistance. Nations will bow to the one and only King Jesus. mdw101920

~

THE DEFINITION OF HOLINESS IS "GIVING NO PLACE TO THE DEVIL." MDW103021

~

Renew your mind in your free time, purge your soul, and let the anointing flow for this preparation of what we are to do. Like Gideon, you run into the battle when the enemy does not expect you. The time of reason is for another season. But standing on the word is more important than from the news you've heard. There should be no compromise to faith in God's faithfulness in your eyes. Display what you have got to make this situation stop. We Are The Redeemed of The Lord.

~

For those who say Jesus has no violence in him and God is all love. He called a woman a dog, rebuked Peter in public, defied Caesar, and said you will not kill me without my permission, for I gave you your power. The angel of God killed Ananias and Sapphira, while God used Paul to strike a man blind. Even God had an angel kill King Herold with worms.

Psalms 86:10 says our God is a mighty warrior. So, do the following scriptures say Our God is a warrior as described in Zephaniah 3:18, Isaiah 42:13, and Habakkuk 3:3-16? I am glad God is on my side, and he fights for me. He is my healer, my provider, my shepherd, my friend, and my protector.

He saves his violence mainly till after he rides a white horse with a sword and sheds blood in the battle of Armageddon up to a horse's bridle and slays millions with his mouth. If you don't know Jesus or your Bible, seek to know him. Will Jesus let you in heaven if you take the mark of the beast? No! He takes away from you what his blood did for you and casts you into the lake of fire. Matthew 11:12 From the days of John the Baptist until now, the kingdom of heaven suffered violence, and the violent take it by force. mdw42320

~

DESIRES DO NOT HAVE TO BE SATISFIED, BUT THEY HAVE TO BE CONTROLLED!32720

~

The place to start for you to win in everything is prayer. Prayer is a voice before the throne of God; prayer is the powerful voice against principalities of darkness with the authority of the name and blood of Jesus. Without prayer, a prophet is weak, a pastor is asleep, an apostle is not respected, an evangelist is rejected, and a teacher is argumentative. Pray is the key to Heaven on Earth and getting people on Earth to Heaven. 32820

~

According to your faith, God will make things right for you to be okay. Fret not of what others do, but lay hold on the destiny God has called you to. His hand is heavy for you to feel, the increase of his Glory you cannot conceal. In boldness in love, you will see a turning point in what you think things should be.

The water in a well shall turn into a stream, and then a river will affect everything. The flood waters of His Glory no one will contain. But an experience that will bring visible, tangible change. You will begin to know his plan, for you will develop your faith, which beyond logic God will use. You will begin to see miracles and healings as angels are disbursed throughout the earth. Souls will be saved as the laborers begin, for endless revivals will begin, regardless of the consent and agreement of men. mdw41620

The proof of what we are made of is in the weight of our commitment, as we are judged, or even how we respond to our offenses should be as Psalms 119:165: "Great Peace have they who love thy law." The pain of my death is what I have to overcome, even as Jesus did.

Apostle Paul made this statement in 2nd Corinthians 4:12. "So, then death works in us so that life in you." The price of being like Jesus is based on sacrifice—choices to not be like the world in one's response during battles and pain.
Death is removal from all life and existence; death is rejection; death is being alone; death is fear; death is pride or self-defense, death to physical and emotional pain; death is hopelessness or even the lack ability of endurance to take place in your life. Being an overcomer is controlling my thoughts to overcome my feelings. Still, Isaiah 53:3-5 tells us of the price Jesus paid in carrying our griefs and sorrows.

3 He is despised and rejected of men;
A man of sorrows, and acquainted with
grief: and we hid as it were our faces from

*him; he was despised, and we esteemed
him not.
4 Surely he hath borne our griefs,
And carried our sorrows:
Yet we did esteem him stricken,
Smitten of God and afflicted.
5 But he was wounded for our
transgressions, he was bruised for our
iniquities: the chastisement of our peace
was upon him; and with his stripes, we
are healed.*

While you still maintain peace and joy as patience rules in your response. The power of faith God has given us is in your words spoken. I'm not moved by how I feel, see, or hear; I'm an overcomer. Only our conflicts manifest what we are. Matthew 18:7...pray that I will arrive...mdw41620

~

Fighting symptoms of sickness is like fighting polluted air. It must be filtered in your thoughts, words, and actions. Faith has a standard beyond logic, for it is the attitude of Heaven, and confidence is expectations of God's word fulfilled. Pain tries to make faith weak and thoughts double-minded.

Your stubborn will can resist or comply. I would rather die in faith than comply with the works of the devil. He steals hope and makes one weary. The power of agreement is imperative in some situations. Fight the good fight of faith. Let me gasp for air as I trust God to breathe into me.

~

Proverbs 3:5. Trust in the Lord with all thine heart; and lean not unto thine own understanding.

~

TRUST SHOULD BE LIKE BREATHING; IF A PROBLEM ARISES, YOU NEED A DOCTOR!

~

DISCIPLINE STARTS IN YOUR THINKING BEFORE MANIFESTING IN YOUR LIFESTYLE AND REACTIONS TO CIRCUMSTANCES! MDW42722

PSALMS 107:20:
"HE SENT HIS WORD AND HEALED YOU AND DELIVERED YOU FROM ALL DESTRUCTION."

Chapter 18
Choice of Commitment

There are wonderful people in our lives who think they need to help change us. Whether it's a wife or husband, family or friends. God is The only one who can change us into the best we can be. His Holy Spirit is working to change you into His image; you cannot get better. So have fun today, and know the potter has his hands on you! 10516

A person of faith is not someone stubborn and foolish but of peace and confidence that allows patience to rule. 101614

Feelings can challenge commitment, but with purpose, it should never be compromised. Purpose is the foundation of commitment; if your responsibility is tired and tempted to quit, remind yourself of purpose. Because if you don't, feelings will try to manipulate you to submitting to a moment and not clinging to the reason of

Purpose!... I John 3:8: "For this purpose came the Son of God, to destroy the works of the devil!...

Since you are still breathing, that means you have not fulfilled your purpose... Many are called, but few are chosen. Stay faithful in the little so that Father God can reward you with much... some plant, some water, and some reap the harvest... Who are you serving? Yourself or God...

~

MEDITATION IS WHAT SECURES WHAT WE KNOW AND WHAT WE BELIEVE.

~

Confidence is the unconscious peace that allows us to do and go beyond logic. When decisions affect others, our confidence should be as our next breath, not a struggle or concern. Know who you are in Christ and who He is to you; eternity is a breath away. Trust should be as taking our next breath.

Priorities start with preference... There is a responsibility, and there is accountability. But the fulfillment of one's heart is linked to enjoyment, anticipation, and application with acceleration because celebration has come into place because of desired accomplishment. 102114

A SMILE IS THE BEGINNING OF LAUGHTER. GO TO THE MIRROR AND SMILE; THE DOOR IS NOW OPENED TO LAUGH AT SITUATIONS BECAUSE YOU

SEE IN YOU THE HOPE NEEDED TO WIN.
102114

~

WHEN LIFE IS HOPELESS, YOU FEED YOUR
HOPE; WHEN ANSWERS ARE FLEETING,
YOU KEEP ASKING QUESTIONS; WHEN
FEAR IS OVERWHELMING, YOU EMBRACE
PEACE; ALL THIS IS IN A MOMENT FOR
THE STEPS OF THOSE WHO REFUSE TO
GIVE IN AND SURRENDER.

~

Everything in life is set to give opportunity to those who fight to have faith in God's faithfulness. Receiving a miracle and receiving an answer to prayer is not while rebelling against your circumstances takes commitment to trust in the Lord and leaning not on your understanding. Proverbs 3:5-6

~

WE ARE LIGHT IN THE DARKNESS, NOT
IN THE DARK WITH NO LIGHT.

~

JESUS IS OUR ANSWER; HE CANNOT LIE;
HIS PROMISES ARE YES AND AMEN. WE
ARE OVERCOMERS BY THE BLOOD OF
THE LAMB AND THE WORDS OF OUR
MOUTH. MDW102112

~

The leaven of the Pharisees (Luke 12:1) was a deception to keep misleading the people with partial truths, which caused the leaders not to be accountable for their lies. In the coming years, the Holiness of God will purge out the pulpit around the earth.

The Chief Shepherd will not allow the under-shepherds to keep leading His sheep astray, as stated in Jeremiah 12:10. For prophetically, John 15 has said the purging and pruning will take place as stated in I Peter 4:7.

The pruning and purging will begin in the leadership of the body of Christ as the presence of God increases, manifestations of signs and wonders are released, and visible encounters with angels will begin and not cease. The war in the heavenlies is over the truth, not control over the earth, because God is alpha and omega.

The Holy Spirit said through Paul in II Thessalonians 2:10,11,12 about many being deceived because they love not the truth. Deception is the misleading of truth. The chance of a lie being fulfilled is like the chance of the truth never being fulfilled. A half-truth is a whole lie. God cannot lie; Jesus is the spotless lamb, which is the way, the truth, and the life. While the Holy Ghost is the Spirit of Truth.

If you do not know the shepherd's voice, you are in a paradigm shift of choice. The comparison of others can be the pivotal point of change that can be the beginning of the misleading of the truth. Many will be deceived because it is what they want to believe, as Paul said, heaping unto themselves teacher that scratches itching ears as stated in II Timothy 4:3.

When Jesus called Satan the father of lies in John 8:44, it is because Satan gave birth to a lie, and there is no truth in a lie other than it's a lie, for a little leaven leavens the whole lump. Except the Lord build the house those that labor; labor in vain as stated in Psalms 127:1.

The Hollywood of ministry will be replaced by the stardom of the overwhelming presence of God, where hours shall turn into days, days turn into weeks, and weeks turn into months. When the river begins to flow, so shall the sovereignty of God we will see and know.

Our days are numbered not in defeat but in a display of God's people taking their seat in the authority of display of who we are and who He is. The light will increase in the midst of the wars that seem not to cease but will come to a sudden end as men and women of God enter into and abide in the Holy of Holies as the body of Christ. We are called to be a triumphant Church. The heavier the anointing, the deeper the revelations. Remember, what you compromise to get, you can ultimately lose. 102217

~

It's not meant for the devil to steal from you, kill you or your family, or destroy you in any way. You can resist the devil, and he must flee. You can bind him, rebuke him, attack him with the sword of the spirit, using the word of God and holding the shield of faith to resist the things the enemy sends at you. You are to wear the helmet of salvation, have your loins rapped with the truth, and your feet having the shoes of righteousness.

We must fight the good fight of faith, trusting in the Lord. Having faith in God's faithfulness while counting it all joy when we fall into all types of temptations, knowing the trying of our faith and the power of patience will cause us to lack for nothing. We are overcomers by the blood of the Lamb and the words of our mouth. So, when you have done all, never surrender to the lies of hell.

The kingdom of Heaven suffers violence, but the violent take it by force. I refuse to surrender my will to demons or those used by demons. I choose to stand on the promises of God and know my redeemed lives, for I am redeemed from the hand of the enemy. For God's plan is for me to be victorious, triumphant, and know he answers prayer, knowing that through faith and patience, I will experience God's promises, for they are yes and amen!

If God be for me, who can control me, not my moment and not those who deny the faith of Jesus in me? I create my future; I refuse to recreate my past. I am a blood-bought child of the King, and no weapon formed against me shall prosper, for the greater one is in me, and if I die in battle, I still win.

~
LOGIC IS NEVER GOD'S SUBJECT!

Chapter 19
Choices Shape
Tomorrow

THE THOUGHTS OF MEN SPEAK LOUDER IN HEAVEN THAN THEIR WORDS ON EARTH!
by William Branham

~

CHOICES ARE NOT ALWAYS IN OUR HANDS, BUT HOLDING ON OR LETTING GO IS! MDW91517

~

Choose your path and walk toward it. Faith may feel like a void, but it sees beyond the clouds and climbs above the problems to rest in the assurance of expectance. Our trust is in the Lord...Proverbs 3:5,6 9-27-17

~

OBEDIENCE IS THE PRIMER TO THE FLOW OF SUPPLY OF ALL YOU HAVE NEED OF!

~

IMMEDIATE OBEDIENCE IS THE DOOR TO
THE MIRACULOUS!

~

PURE OBEDIENCE IS NEVER A SACRIFICE!

~

DESIRE AMPLIFIES ABILITY, AND
DISCIPLINE INCREASES RESULTS!

~

THE VOID OF TOMORROW CAN BE
FILLED BY THE CHOICES OF TODAY.
MDW122317

~

Choose your path and walk toward it. Faith may feel
like a void, but it sees beyond the clouds and climbs
above the problems to rest in the assurance of
expectance. Our trust is in the Lord. Proverbs
3:5,6...mdw92717

~

Integrity is a choice... being responsible is a choice...
lying is a choice...being honest with yourself is
integrity...don't lie to yourself... Your future is in
your hands with your choices.

~

YOU WILL BE DECEIVED IF YOU DON'T
LOVE TRUTH MORE THAN YOU LOVE
PEOPLE! MDW4320

~

Mental pressure can be a motivational change from
others. I know that because of family and friends,
the pressure to conform to others' ideas and not
one's own conscience. My eternity is based on my

conscience and my relationship with Jesus. When I am at the judgment seat, I will be judged for my choices, not what others make or try to make for me.

~

Running from a battle is running from victory. Running from what people say about you is running from vindication. Life is full of battles, but victories are only to those who stand on principles of truth, not parallels of people's opinions. Remember, your eternity is based totally on you individually and what you believe, not what others think. So, when you have done all, stand your ground because a smile from Heaven does not remove the frown of carnal men.

~

So, People with short tempers have the sign of little love, little peace, and little patience and need much time with God. But they don't seek God much because God doesn't jump when they say jump! mdw41814

~

Renew your mind in your free time, purge your soul, and let the anointing flow for this preparation of what we are to do. Like Gideon, you run into the battle when the enemy does not expect you. The time of reason is for another season. But standing on the word is more important than from the news you've heard. There should be no compromise to faith in God's faithfulness in your eyes. So, display what you have got to make this situation stop. We are the "Redeemed of The Lord," so say so and act so. 42020

THINGS TO PURSUE FOR GOD TO USE YOU

What Increases the Anointing in Your Life?
- Integrity
- Purity & Holiness
- Having a Vision of Purpose
- Hunger
- Crucify
- Prayer Life
- Fruit of the Spirit - Attitude
- Loving like Jesus
- Humility
- Being a Servant
- Being a Doer of the Word
- Compassion for others
- Immediate Obedience
- Can God Trust You
- Have a Strong, Committed Faith

~

THE EMOTIONS OF ONE'S FLESH CAN SUMMON UP FALSE REALITIES, WHICH CAN CAUSE THE BLIND TO LEAD THE BLIND, WHILE THOSE WHO FALL INTO THE DITCH WILL FIND IT DIFFICULT TO GET BACK INTO THE STRAIGHT AND NARROW PATH OF RIGHTEOUSNESS.

~

THE FRUIT OF YOUR LIPS COMES FROM THE SEED OF YOUR THOUGHTS!

~

Chapter 20
The Price of Value

John 3:16,17

16 For God so loved the world, that he gave his only begotten Son, that whosoever believeth in him should not perish, but have everlasting life. 17 For God sent not his Son into the world to condemn the world; but that the world through him might be saved.!

~

et us talk about the price of value. In the book of Matthew 13:44, "Again, the kingdom of heaven is like unto treasure hid in a field; the which when a man hath found, he hideth, and for joy thereof goeth and selleth all that he hath, and buyeth that field."

Whatever this man found was a treasure to him. It is possible that what was found could be a gemstone or even gold. He had to dig for it. Whatever he found, he sold all to embrace what was valuable to him.

In Matthew 13:45,46, "Again, the kingdom of heaven is like unto a merchant man, seeking goodly pearls: [46] who, when he had found one pearl of great price, went and sold all that he had, and bought it."

The path of pearls is a long, time-consuming experience. There are raw pearls and cultured pearls. Systematic applications by man cause one type, and the other is created by the hand of God. Both require time, patience, and oversight. The most expensive one is what is called raw pearls. This was made by the hand of God through a creation process.

Pearls are developed by an irritation getting inside an oyster. The irritations can be bacteria or sand that gets trapped between the mantle folds, and in time, with consistent application, the irritant is covered again and again while what hurt inside is made smooth. Time causes a beautiful round, shiny white or black object, which is a priceless treasure to all of humanity, to be created as a jeweler's luster with a distinctive glow because of a duration of continuous overcoming an irritant.

THE PRICE OF YOUR FUTURE IS PAID
WITH THE INVESTMENTS OF YOUR
TODAY!

WHEN TIME CONTROLS YOUR DESTINY, WHAT DO YOU DO IN YOUR SPARE TIME?

~

IF YOU LIVE OFF EXCUSES, YOU CAN DIE BECAUSE OF THE REASONS.

Patience is the strength of my tomorrow. Patience is the hope of my future, the dream of my desires. For without Patience, I have no Peace. It is with faith and patience that we obtain the promise. (Hebrews 6:12) Patience is not just a frame of mind, but an attitude maintained over time.

~

It might take years to get somewhere in life, accomplishments reaching, goals, and education. But then, it's gone in a moment by making wrong decisions or listening to logical counsel, not spiritual. But you started with a moment to get where you are at, so press in and start again and again and again. Winners never quit, and quitters never win. Winning is inside out before it is ever outside in! You might have Fallen or Failed but Never Defeated!

This is the last paragraph in the last chapter of my latest book "Foundational Roots Imparting Success."

Renew your mind in your free time, purge your soul, and let the anointing flow. For this preparation of what we are to do. Running into the battle, like

Gideon, when the enemy does not expect you. The time of reason is for another season.

But standing on the word is more important than the news you've heard. There should be no compromise to faith in God's faithfulness in your eyes. So, display what you have got to make this situation stop. We Are The Redeemed of The Lord.

~

PSALMS 107:20
HE SENT HIS WORD AND HEALED THEM AND DELIVERED THEM FROM THEIR DESTRUCTION.

~

"Omnia Vincit Amor," or love conquers all, was first introduced by the Roman poet Virgil in his tenth Eclogue, published around 37 B.C. Learn how to love like God. Learn how to love beyond logic!

~

KNOW THIS: A MISTAKE IN A MOMENT CAN TAKE AWAY FROM YOU WHAT IT TOOK YEARS TO EARN. BE ALERT, BE CAUTIOUS, GIVE NO PLACE TO THE DEVIL.

Chapter 21

Responding to your ability

"RESPONDING TO YOUR ABILITY, IS YOUR RESPONSIBILITY!"

The baptism of the Holy Spirit with the evidence of speaking in tongues is one of the great promises the Bible gives in the New Testament to believers (Mark 16:17)

Daily praying in the Spirit can return many tremendous benefits of the believer who desires a genuine relationship with Jesus and personal victory in every area of one's life here on earth.

Below is a list of scriptures most productive by praying often and in the Spirit.

1. I Cor. 14:4 Praying in the Spirit keeps you personally encouraged.

2. I Cor. 14:2 Praying in the Spirit keeps you sensitive to the voice of God.

3. II Corinthians 3:17 Praying in the Spirit keeps you confident in yourself.

4. Romans 5:5 Praying daily in the Spirit causes you to walk in love.

5. Romans 8:26-27 Praying in the Spirit helps you get answers to your prayers.

6. Jude 20 Builds and strengthens your faith in the word and spirit of God.

7. Acts 1:8 Having prowess in the spirit comes from praying the Spirit.

8. John 16:13 Praying in the spirit ignites the fire of God in you as the Word comes alive.

Below are scriptures for guidance.

1 Corinthians 3:8
He who plants and he who waters are one, and each will receive his wages according to his labor.

Proverbs 22:6
Train up a child in the way he should go; even when he is old, he will not depart from it.

1 Corinthians 13:11
When I was a child, I spoke like a child, I thought like a child, I reasoned like a child. When I became a man, I gave up childish ways.

1 John 1:9
If we confess our sins, he is faithful and just to forgive us our sins and to cleanse us from all unrighteousness.

2 Corinthians 5:10
For we must all appear before the judgment seat of Christ, so that each one may receive what is due for what he has done in the body, whether good or evil.

2 Timothy 1:7
For God gave us a spirit not of fear but of power and love and self-control.

Colossians 3:23
Whatever you do, work heartily, as for the Lord and not for men.

Ephesians 6:4
Fathers, do not provoke your children to anger but bring them up in the discipline and instruction of the Lord.

Galatians 6:2
Bear one another's burdens, and so fulfill the law of Christ.

Galatians 6:7
Do not be deceived: God is not mocked, for whatever one sows, that will he also reap.

Genesis 16:5
And Sarai said to Abram, "May the wrong done to me be on you! I gave my servant to your embrace, and when she saw that she had conceived, she looked at me with contempt. May the Lord judge between you and me!"

~

RESPONSIBILITY WAS ADAM'S TO GUARD AND PROTECT, BUT HE DID NOT. HE TOOK THE PASSIVE ROUTE, AS DID AHAB WITH JEZABEL.

James 4:17
So whoever knows the right thing to do and fails to do it, for him, it is sin.

James 4:7
Submit yourselves therefore to God. Resist the devil, and he will flee from you.

John 12:48
"The one who rejects me and does not receive my words has a judge; the word that I have spoken will judge him on the last day."

John 15:22
"If I had not come and spoken to them, they would not have been guilty of sin, but now they have no

excuse for their sin."

Luke 12:48
"But the one who did not know and did what deserved a beating will receive a light beating. Everyone to whom much was given, of him much will be required, and from him to whom they entrusted much, they will demand the more."

Luke 16:10
"One who is faithful in a very little is also faithful in much, and one who is dishonest in a very little is also dishonest in much."

Matthew 12:37
"For by your words you will be justified, and by your words you will be condemned."

Matthew 27:24
So when Pilate saw that he was gaining nothing, but rather that a riot was beginning, he took water and washed his hands before the crowd, saying, "I am innocent of this man's blood; see to it yourselves."

Proverbs 28:13
Whoever conceals his transgressions will not prosper, but he who confesses and forsakes them will obtain mercy.

Proverbs 6:6
Go to the ant, O sluggard; consider her ways, and be wise.

Romans 12:3
For by the grace given to me, I say to everyone among you not to think of himself more highly than he ought to think, but to think with sober judgment, each according to the measure of faith that God has assigned.

Romans 14:1
As for the one who is weak in faith, welcome him, but do not quarrel over opinions.

Romans 14:12
So then, each of us will give an account of himself to God.

~

LOGIC IS NEVER GOD'S SUBJECT!

~

PEOPLE QUICK TO JUDGE ARE SLOW TO SAY I WAS WRONG!

Ezekiel 3:17-21

[17] Son of man, I have made thee a watchman unto the house of Israel: therefore hear the word at my mouth, and give them warning from me.

[18] When I say unto the wicked, Thou shalt surely die; and thou givest him not warning, nor speakest to warn the wicked from his wicked way, to save his life; the same wicked man shall die in his iniquity; but his blood will I require at thine hand.

[19] Yet if thou warn the wicked, and he turn not from his wickedness, nor from his wicked way, he shall die in his iniquity; but thou hast delivered thy soul.

[20] Again, When a righteous man doth turn from his righteousness, and commit iniquity, and I lay a stumbling-block before him, he shall die: because thou hast not given him warning, he shall die in his sin, and his righteousness which he hath done shall not be remembered; but his blood will I require at thine hand.

[21] Nevertheless if thou warn the righteous man, that the righteous sin not, and he doth not sin, he shall surely live, because he is warned; also thou hast delivered thy soul.

BIOGRAPHY OF
DR. MARK D. WHITE
EXPRESSING THE FATHER'S HEART!

 Mark D. White was raised as an Assembly of God pastor's son and started preaching at 15. In 1978, he graduated from Kenneth E. Hagin's Rhema Bible Training Center in Tulsa, Oklahoma.   Since then, he has been an associate pastor of two churches and has pastored three. Mark also holds a Doctorate from Saint Thomas University and a BS/BM from the University of Phoenix.

Mark travels extensively throughout the United States and travels internationally, ministering the Word of God by precept and example. Having over 50 years of active experience in ministry gives place to the workings of the Holy Spirit in the lives of believers and unbelievers. Mark's insight and practical understanding of the spirit allows him to operate in the Prophet's office with a pastor's heart. There is a strong anointing upon him, which gives place to the open move of the Holy Spirit in strengthening the local church.

Mark has a reputation for balanced teaching and preaching with compassion for the heart of the people. Homes are restored, blind eyes are opened, deaf ears are healed, cancer disappears, cataracts are removed, and broken hearts are mended. The Word of God is preached with signs following. Miracles and Healings happen in every service. Mark desires to serve the purpose of every local church and ministry.

www.markwhite.tv

www.rapha.us

Email address – rapha@gmx.us

Here are other books written by
Dr. Mark D. White

YOUR IDENTITY

THE THUMBPRINT OF GOD

Dr. Mark D. White

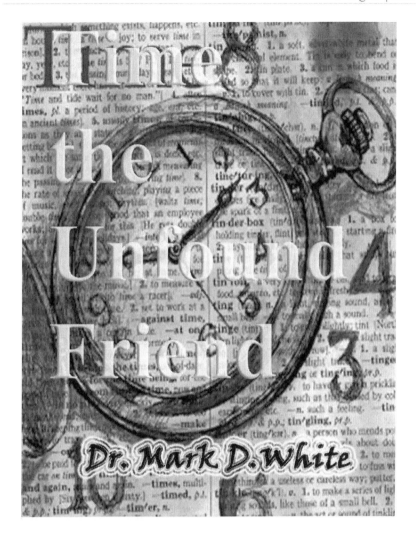

FOUNDATIONAL ROOTS
FOR SUCCESS

DR. MARK D. WHITE

FORWARD BY
DR. MARK & HELEN DUPLANTIS
AND DR. JEFF JANSEN

PSALMS 107:20: "HE SENT HIS WORD AND HEALED YOU AND DELIVERED YOU FROM ALL DESTRUCTION."

Invitation for a prayer of accepting Jesus Christ as Lord and Savior.

Father God, Creator of the Universe. In the name of Jesus, I am asking you to accept me into your family as a child of God. I believe that Jesus Christ is your son, and he was born of a virgin, died on the cross, and you raised him from the dead. Jesus became sin so I could stand right before the Throne of God because of the blood that Jesus shed for me. I ask you to forgive me for all I have done wrong, and I ask that Jesus come into my heart and be my Lord and Savior. I now confess that Jesus Christ is my Lord, and I am now born again. I ask that the Holy Spirit lead me and teach me to have a daily relationship with you.

I recommend reading the Bible daily. At the same time, I meditate on Matthew's, Mark's, Luke's, and John's books about Jesus's life.

WELCOME TO THE FAMILY OF GOD!

Made in the USA
Columbia, SC
29 October 2024

44988089R00100